WELCOME TO MEDITERRANEAN DIET COOKBOOK

for beginners

Disclaimer

The information in this book is provided for general informational purposes only. It is not intended as, nor should it be considered a substitute for, professional medical advice, diagnosis, or treatment. Always seek the advice of your physician or other qualified health provider with any questions you may have regarding a medical condition.

The author and publisher disclaim any liability or responsibility to any person or entity for any loss, damage, or adverse consequences alleged to have happened directly or indirectly due to material in this book.

Individual nutritional needs and restrictions can vary; it is advised to consult with a healthcare professional or registered dietitian before making significant changes to your diet. The recipes and recommendations in this book are based on the author's experience and research, but results may vary and are not guaranteed.

All brand names and trademarks mentioned in this book are the property of their respective owners. We include these brand names and trademarks solely for the purpose of providing a comprehensive understanding of the health and nutrition landscape. The inclusion of these brand names and trademarks is not intended to imply endorsement or affiliation with the author or publisher.

hello there
I'M SOPHIE

I'm thrilled to welcome you to "The Mediterranean Diet Cookbook for Beginners." For years, I have been passionate about cooking and healthy living, and I discovered the Mediterranean diet as a game-changer. This is not just another diet but a lifestyle rooted in vibrant, flavorful foods that nourish your body and soul.

My personal connection with the Mediterranean diet began during a memorable trip to Greece. The local cuisine, with its focus on fresh, wholesome ingredients, left a lasting impression on me. Since then, I've been on a mission to create and refine Mediterranean recipes that are both delicious and easy to prepare. This cookbook is a testament to my journey, filled with recipes that are perfect for anyone seeking a healthier lifestyle without compromising on taste.

Whether you're a seasoned cook or just starting out in the kitchen, these recipes are simple, approachable, and incredibly rewarding. I hope this book inspires you to embrace the Mediterranean way of eating and brings a bit of sunshine and flavor into your everyday meals.

Happy cooking!

Sophie Armstrong

table of
CONTENTS

00   INTRODUCTION..9

01   GET STARTED...11

02   CHAPTER. BREAKFASTS.................................12

      MEDITERRANEAN OATMEAL.................................13

      TOMATO AND FETA TOAST.................................14

      GREEK YOGURT WITH NUTS AND HONEY.................15

      EGG SCRAMBLE WITH SPINACH.........................16

      SWEET PEA AND RICOTTA TOAST.....................17

      MUESLI WITH SKYR.......................................18

      SAVORY MUFFIN WITH OLIVES AND FETA 19

      SIMPLE SHAKSHUKA.....................................20

      TURKISH MENEMEN.......................................21

      MEDITERRANEAN EGG MUFFINS,,,,,,,,,,,,,,,,,,,,,,,,.....22

03   CHAPTER. SNACKS AND APPETIZERS....................23

      GREEK YOGURT AND CUCUMBER DIP (TZATZIKI).......24

      CLASSIC HUMMUS.......................................25

      BRUSCHETTA WITH TOMATO AND BASIL.................26

      CAPRESE SKEWERS.......................................27

ZUCCHINI FRITTERS..............................28

GRILLED HALLOUMI..............................29

MEDITERRANEAN DEVILED EGGS..............................30

TAPENADE..............................31

MUSHROOM AND GOAT CHEESE CROSTINI..............................32

ROASTED RED PEPPER HUMMUS..............................33

PISTACHIO AND POMEGRANATE MUHAMMARA..............................34

SMOKED SALMON AND CREAM CHEESE ROLLS..............................35

04 CHAPTER. SALADS..............................36

GREEK VILLAGE SALAD (HORIATIKI)..............................37

TABBOULEH..............................38

WATERMELON AND FETA SALAD..............................39

CHICKPEA AND SPINACH SALAD..............................40

MEDITERRANEAN BEET SALAD..............................41

CUCUMBER AND YOGURT SALAD (CACIK)..............................42

ROASTED PEPPER AND ARTICHOKE SALAD..............................43

FIG AND ARUGULA SALAD..............................44

MEDITERRANEAN CAULIFLOWER SALAD..............................45

AVOCADO AND QUINOA SALAD..............................46

BROCCOLI AND CHICKPEA SALAD..............................47

GRILLED CALAMARI SALAD..............................48

05 CHAPTER. SOUPS..49

    CLASSIC MINESTRONE SOUP..............................50

    LENTIL AND SPINACH SOUP..............................51

    GREEK LEMON CHICKEN SOUP (AVGOLEMONO)......52

    MEDITERRANEAN VEGETABLE SOUP.....................53

    CHICKPEA AND TOMATO SOUP..........................54

    TUSCAN WHITE BEAN SOUP..............................55

    ROASTED RED PEPPER AND TOMATO SOUP............56

    MEDITERRANEAN FISH SOUP.............................57

    SPICY MOROCCAN LENTIL SOUP.........................58

    CREAMY CAULIFLOWER AND GARLIC SOUP............59

    SPANISH GAZPACHO.......................................60

    HEARTY BARLEY AND MUSHROOM SOUP................61

06 CHAPTER. FISH AND SEAFOOD..........................62

    GRILLED SALMON WITH LEMON AND DILL..............63

    SHRIMP SAGANAKI..64

    MEDITERRANEAN BAKED COD...........................65

    SEAFOOD PAELLA...66

    BAKED RED SNAPPER.....................................67

    BAKED COD WITH TOMATOES AND OLIVES............68

    SALMON AND ASPARAGUS...............................69

    BAKED TILAPIA WITH LEMON...........................70

FISH AND VEGETABLE SKEWERS...............................71

LEMON GARLIC MUSSELS...............................72

GRILLED SWORDFISH STEAKS...............................73

PAN-SEARED SCALLOPS...............................74

07 CHAPTER. MAIN DISHES...............................75

GREEK CHICKEN SOUVLAKI...............................76

GARLIC AND HERB GRILLED LAMB CHOPS.................77

ITALIAN SHRIMP PASTA...............................78

ITALIAN CAPRESE STUFFED PEPPERS...........................79.

ITALIAN MOROCCAN RED LENTIL AND PUMPKIN STEW...............................80

FARRO WITH ROASTED TOMATOES AND MUSHROOMS...............................81

STUFFED PORTOBELLOS...............................82

CREAMY CHICKPEA SAUCE WITH WHOLE-WHEAT FUSILLI...............................83

ROASTED VEGETABLE AND HUMMUS WRAP.............84

MEDITERRANEAN BAKED CHICKEN THIGHS..............85

MEDITERRANEAN STUFFED ZUCCHINI BOATS..........86

MEDITERRANEAN RATATOUILLE...............................87

08 CHAPTER. DESSERTS..88

POACHED PEARS IN RED WINE...............................89

BAKED APPLES WITH CINNAMON AND HONEY....90

GRILLED PEACHES WITH GREEK YOGURT.............91

BERRY AND MINT SALAD..92

BAKED FIGS WITH HONEY AND ALMONDS.............93

OLIVE OIL AND ALMOND CAKE..............................94

RICOTTA AND HONEY TARTLETS...........................95

DARK CHOCOLATE-COVERED ALMONDS.............96

OLIVE OIL COOKIES...97

MEDITERRANEAN ORANGE YOGURT CAKE..........98

09 CHAPTER. SAUCES AND CONDIMENTS....................99

ZATZIKI..100

CLASSIC BASIL PESTO...101

TAPENADE...102

MUHAMMARA...103

ROMESCO...104

MEAL PLAN ADVICES...105

30-DAY MEAL PLAN..106

COOKING CONVERSION CHART............................108

CONCLUSION...110

Introduction
OVERVIEW OF THE MEDITERRANEAN DIET

The Mediterranean diet is one of the best diets in the world. It is a long-term, all-encompassing eating style that includes nutritious food, spending time with loved ones, regular exercise, and practicing mindfulness.

The rich, savory culinary traditions and myriad health benefits of the Mediterranean diet are widely acknowledged. This diet is mainly based on the eating habits of the Mediterranean Sea-bordering nations of Greece, Italy, and Spain. The primary source of fat is olive oil, and it is emphasized to consume whole grains, fruits, vegetables, legumes, nuts, and seeds. Along with modest intakes of dairy, red meat, and sweets, this diet also calls for moderate amounts of fish and poultry.

More than just a list of foods, the Mediterranean diet refers to a way of eating that is ingrained in the customs and culture of the Mediterranean region:

• Social Eating: People generally see meals as an opportunity to socialize and unwind rather than just as a means of consuming food.

• Seasonal and Fresh Foods: Eating foods that are in season and sourced locally is prioritized.

• Physical Activity: Besides diet, regular physical activity is essential to lifestyle.

The customary eating patterns of the Mediterranean people serve as the foundation for the Mediterranean diet. Among the fundamental ideas are:

Plant-Based Foods

An abundance of fruits, vegetables, whole grains, nuts, and legumes form the cornerstone of this diet. High in fiber and other nutrients, these foods are eaten in large quantities daily.

Heart-healthy Fats

Olive oil, well-known for its heart-healthy qualities, is the primary source of added fat. It's a common ingredient in cooking and salad dressings. Nuts, peanuts, and avocados are additional sources of good fats.

Moderate Protein Intake

Fish and seafood contain omega-3 fatty acids and high-quality protein, which should be consumed at least twice weekly. Red meat is consumed less frequently than poultry, eggs, and dairy items (such as cheese and yogurt), all of which should be eaten in moderation.

Herbs and Spices

A range of herbs and spices are used to flavor meals in place of salt, lowering sodium intake and improving the flavor profile of the dishes.

Wine

Many people in the area prefer drinking red wine in moderation, usually with meals, which adds to the nutritional advantages of this eating pattern.

WHY IT IS GREAT FOR BEGINNERS

Starting a new diet might be intimidating, but the Mediterranean Diet provides a friendly and straightforward route for those new to it. This diet is well-known for its easy adoption and numerous health benefits, making it an excellent option for anyone beginning their gastronomic wellness journey. Three factors make the Mediterranean Diet a perfect choice for novices.

Simpleness of the Dinners

The ease with which the meals on the Mediterranean Diet are prepared is among its most alluring features. This diet emphasizes using complete, unprocessed foods that you can make with a minimum amount of culinary expertise instead of diets that call for unusual ingredients or intricate cooking techniques. Fresh veggies, fruits, whole grains, nuts, and olive oil may be mixed in various ways to make tasty, healthful meals. For instance, grilled fish, sautéed vegetables on the side, and a basic salad may make up a regular supper. These dishes are simple to make but incredibly flavorful and nutrient-dense.

Ingredient Availability

Beginners will find the Mediterranean Diet convenient because the staple items are readily available in most stores. Fresh herbs, garlic, olive oil, tomatoes, and other culinary mainstays are highlighted in this diet. Because these ingredients are readily available, you can begin this diet without looking for specialized retailers. Because many essential components are readily available and reasonably priced, this availability also contributes to maintaining a budget-friendly approach to healthy eating.

Flexibility in the Planning of Meals

The Mediterranean Diet's flexibility is a significant draw for beginners. With no strict meal timings or calorie intake rules, novice dieters can tailor the diet to their schedules and preferences. Whether you're a busy professional or a parent juggling multiple responsibilities, you can find ways to incorporate the diet's principles into your daily routine. The diet encourages variety and moderation, allowing you to enjoy various foods and even the occasional red wine.

In summary

It's possible to begin the Mediterranean diet smoothly and with pleasure. It introduces newcomers to a sustainable eating style that can improve their palate and health with straightforward dishes, quickly accessible products, and adaptable meal planning. Selecting the Mediterranean Diet means accepting a way of life that values health, happiness, and delicious food rather than merely picking up a new diet. Discover quick, tasty recipes and helpful advice to help you get started on the Mediterranean diet with confidence and enjoyment by diving into the Mediterranean Diet Cookbook for Beginners.

Chapter 01
GET STARTED

Setting Up Your Mediterranean Kitchen

Initiate a Mediterranean-inspired gastronomic adventure in your kitchen. To master the Mediterranean diet, stock your pantry with essentials, outfit your cooking area with the necessary tools, and locate the best ingredients. This book makes all of these tasks easier

Essential Kitchen Tools and Equipment

• A well-stocked kitchen is essential for efficiently preparing Mediterranean cuisine. First, you'll need a decent pair of knives for chopping fresh herbs and veggies. Purchase a set of mixing bowls and a solid chopping board; for recipes like Italian pasta and Spanish paellas, a big pot and a good skillet are essential. Fresh garlic is a critical component of Mediterranean cooking, so invest in a garlic press and grater for fresh cheese and citrus zest. Finally, since this diet is heavy on fresh greens, consider getting a salad spinner.

.

Pantry Staples

The pantry is the heart of a Mediterranean kitchen, filled with essential ingredients that bring the flavors of the Mediterranean to your table. Here are several necessities.

Olive oil

Use extra-virgin olive oil when dressing and completing dishes. It enhances the flavor of your food and is also a heart-healthy fat, providing reassurance about your dietary choices.

Herbs and spices

Keep dried mint, basil, rosemary, oregano, and thyme on hand. These are adaptable and suitable for a wide range of recipes. Remember to add cumin and saffron for a hint of exotic flavor.

Grains

You should keep a special place in your cupboard for whole grains like couscous, bulgur, farro, and pasta.

Legumes

White beans, lentils, and chickpeas are excellent protein sources for your diet.

Nuts and seeds

Sesame seeds, pine nuts, and almonds make delicious snacks or crunchy additions to salads.

Vinegar with citrus

Fresh lemons and limes work well with red and balsamic wine vinegar for bright marinades and salads..

Shopping List and Sourcing Quality Ingredients

Freshness counts when purchasing ingredients. Visit your local farmer's markets to find the freshest fruits and veggies. Check out respectable fish markets or speak with your neighborhood grocer about responsibly sourced seafood. Choose meats raised on pasture or in a free-range environment to guarantee high quality and moral treatment.

Although dried herbs might be helpful in situations outside of the growing season, fresh herbs are preferable. For pantry staples like spices and olive oil, look for specialty shops or internet merchants with a reputation for high-quality goods. It's essential to read labels since genuine components equal genuine flavors carefully.

CHAPTER 02
Breakfasts

MEDITERRANEAN OATMEAL

SERVES
4

PREP TIME
10

METHOD
Simmering

COOK TIME
10

DIRECTIONS

1. Boil the water in a medium pot. After adding the salt and rolled oats, lower the heat to low and cook, stirring periodically, until the oats become tender about 5 minutes.
2. Add the chopped walnuts, cinnamon, honey, and dried figs. Reduce heat and cook for a further five minutes.
3. Turn off the heat and leave the oatmeal alone for two minutes to thicken.
4. Top the porridge with freshly chopped basil and crumbled feta cheese.

INGREDIENTS

- 2 cups rolled oats.
- 4 cups water
- 1/2 teaspoon salt
- 1/4 cup chopped dried figs.
- 1/4 cup chopped walnuts.

- 2 tablespoons honey
- 1/2 teaspoon ground cinnamon
- 1/4 cup crumbled feta cheese
- 1/4 cup fresh chopped basil

NUTRITIONAL INFORMATION

290 calories, 8 g protein, 49 g carbohydrates, 9 g fat, 6 g fiber, 8 mg cholesterol, 310 mg sodium, 270 mg potassium.

TOMATO AND FETA TOAST

SERVES
4

PREP TIME
10

METHOD
Toasting

COOK TIME
5

DIRECTIONS

1. Place the sourdough pieces on a baking tray and preheat your broiler to high. Apply a thin layer of olive oil to every slice.
2. Top each slice of bread with sliced tomatoes and a dash of salt and pepper.
3. Scatter the amount of feta cheese crumbles evenly on top of the tomatoes.
4. Place in the broiler for three to five minutes or until the feta melts and the bread is toasted to your preference.
5. Remove it from the broiler, top with freshly chopped basil, and drizzle some balsamic glaze before serving.

INGREDIENTS

- 4 slices of sourdough bread
- 2 large tomatoes, sliced.
- 1 cup crumbled feta cheese
- 1/4 cup fresh basil leaves, chopped.
- 2 tablespoons olive oil
- Salt and pepper to taste
- Optional: balsamic glaze for drizzling

NUTRITIONAL INFORMATION

250 calories, 9 g protein, 27 g carbohydrates, 12 g fat, 2 g fiber, 25 mg cholesterol, 580 mg sodium, 210 mg potassium

GREEK YOGURT WITH NUTS AND HONEY

SERVES
4

PREP TIME
5

METHOD
NO-COOK

COOK TIME
0

DIRECTIONS

1. Evenly distribute the Greek yogurt among four dishes.
2. Top each dish of yogurt with a sprinkle of chopped almonds.
3. Drizzle one tablespoon of honey over each serving.
4. For extra taste, sprinkle ground cinnamon on the nuts and honey.

INGREDIENTS

- 2 cups plain Greek yogurt
- 1/4 cup mixed nuts (such as almonds, walnuts, and pistachios) roughly chopped.
- 4 tablespoons honey
- 1/2 teaspoon ground cinnamon

NUTRITIONAL INFORMATION

200 calories, 10 g protein, 18 g carbohydrates, 8 g fat, 1 g fiber, 10 mg cholesterol, 45 mg sodium, 200 mg potassium.

EGG SCRAMBLE WITH SPINACH

SERVES
4

PREP TIME
5

METHOD
Sautéing

COOK TIME
10

DIRECTIONS

1. Combine the eggs, milk, pepper, and salt in a bowl. Put aside.
2. In a big skillet over medium heat, preheat the olive oil. Add the chopped onion and cook for about 3 minutes or until transparent.
3. Add the spinach to the skillet and simmer for two minutes or until it has barely wilted.
4. Cover the onions and spinach with the egg mixture. After letting it sit for about a minute without moving, give it a little swirl and scramble the eggs for approximately five minutes or until they are softly set with some runny spots.
5. Top the eggs with grated cheddar cheese and let it melt. Remove from the heat and serve right away.

INGREDIENTS

- 8 large eggs
- 1/2 cup milk
- 1/4 teaspoon salt
- 1/4 teaspoon black pepper
- 2 tablespoons olive oil

- 1 small onion finely chopped.
- 2 cups fresh spinach roughly chopped.
- 1/2 cup shredded cheddar cheese

NUTRITIONAL INFORMATION

290 calories, 19 g protein, 5 g carbohydrates, 22 g fat, 1 g fiber, 390 mg cholesterol, 430 mg sodium, 340 mg potassium

SWEET PEA AND RICOTTA TOAST

DIRECTIONS

1. Thaw frozen peas if using them. The peas should be softly cooked in a small saucepan of boiling water for about two minutes. Empty and leave to cool.
2. Place the ricotta cheese, lemon juice, zest, salt, and black pepper in a bowl. Blend thoroughly by mixing.
3. Toast the bread slices until they are the right color.
4. Evenly distribute the ricotta mixture on every toast slice. Add cooked peas, a little olive oil, and some chopped mint.

SERVES
4

PREP TIME
5

METHOD
Toasting

COOK TIME
10

INGREDIENTS

- 1 cup fresh or frozen peas
- 4 slices of whole grain bread
- 1 cup ricotta cheese
- 1/2 lemon zested and juiced.
- 1/4 teaspoon salt
- 1/4 teaspoon black pepper
- 2 tablespoons extra virgin olive oil
- 2 tablespoons chopped fresh mint.

NUTRITIONAL INFORMATION

280 calories, 12 g protein, 29 g carbohydrates, 14 g fat, 5 g fiber, 31 mg cholesterol, 390 mg sodium, 220 mg potassium.

MUESLI WITH SKYR

SERVES
4

PREP TIME
10

METHOD
NO-COOK

COOK TIME
0

DIRECTIONS

1. Place rolled oats, chopped almonds, raisins, dried cranberries, pumpkin seeds, and ground cinnamon in a big mixing dish.
2. Combine Skyr, almond milk, and honey in another bowl and whisk until smooth.
3. Cover the oat mixture with the Skyr mixture and stir until thoroughly mixed. To let the flavors to mingle and the oats to soften, cover and refrigerate overnight.
4. If preferred, top chilled serving with fresh berries.

INGREDIENTS

- 2 cups rolled oats.
- 1/4 cup sliced almonds.
- 1/4 cup dried cranberries
- 1/4 cup raisins
- 2 tablespoons pumpkin seeds
- 1/4 teaspoon ground cinnamon

- 2 cups Skyr (Icelandic yogurt)
- 1 cup almond milk
- 2 tablespoons honey
- Fresh berries for topping (optional)

NUTRITIONAL INFORMATION

370 calories, 22 g protein, 53 g carbohydrates, 9 g fat, 7 g fiber, 10 mg cholesterol, 95 mg sodium, 350 mg potassium.

18

SAVORY MUFFINS WITH OLIVES AND FETA

SERVES
6

PREP TIME
15

METHOD
Baking

COOK TIME
20

DIRECTIONS

1. Preheat the oven to 375°F (190°C). Grease or line a 12-cup muffin tray with paper cups.
2. Combine the flour, baking powder, salt, and black pepper in a sizable bowl. Beat the eggs, milk, and olive oil together until smooth in a another bowl.
3. Add the wet mixture to the dry mixture and whisk until blended. Stir in the chopped basil, feta cheese, and olives.
4. Transfer the batter into the muffin tins, filling each to approximately three-quarters of the way to the top. A toothpick put into the center of a muffin should come out clean after 20 minutes of baking in a preheated oven or until the tops are brown.
5. After the muffins have cooled in the pan for five minutes, move them to a wire rack to finish cooling.

INGREDIENTS

- 2 cups all-purpose flour
- 1 tablespoon baking powder
- 1/2 teaspoon salt
- 1/2 teaspoon black pepper
- 2 large eggs
- 1 cup milk
- 1/4 cup olive oil
- 1/2 cup crumbled feta cheese
- 1/2 cup chopped pitted kalamata olives.
- 1/4 cup finely chopped fresh basil.

NUTRITIONAL INFORMATION

300 calories, 9 g protein, 35 g carbohydrates, 14 g fat, 2 g fiber, 55 mg cholesterol, 540 mg sodium, 160 mg potassium.

SIMPLE SHAKSHUKA

SERVES
4

PREP TIME
15

METHOD
Sautéing

COOK TIME
25

DIRECTIONS

1. In a big skillet over medium heat, warm the olive oil. Add the bell pepper and onion, and cook for about 5 minutes or until tender. Add the chili powder, paprika, cumin, and garlic; simmer for two minutes or until fragrant.

2. Add the chopped tomatoes and their liquids and stir. Add pepper and salt for seasoning. Simmer the tomato mixture for about 15 minutes or until it thickens somewhat.

3. Using a spoon, make little wells in the sauce and crack one egg into each well. For about five to seven minutes, or when the egg whites are set but the yolks are still runny, cover the skillet and cook the egg.

4. Turn off the heat, sprinkle with chopped parsley or cilantro, and serve right out of the skillet.

INGREDIENTS

- 2 tablespoons olive oil
- 1 medium onion, chopped.
- 1 red bell pepper, chopped.
- 3 cloves garlic, minced.
- 1 teaspoon paprika
- 1 teaspoon ground cumin
- 1/4 teaspoon chili powder

- 1 (28-ounce) can whole peeled tomatoes, coarsely chopped
- Salt and pepper to taste
- 6 large eggs
- Fresh cilantro or parsley for garnish

NUTRITIONAL INFORMATION

235 calories, 12 g protein, 17 g carbohydrates, 14 g fat, 5 g fiber, 372 mg cholesterol, 408 mg sodium, 589 mg potassium.

TURKISH MENEMEN

SERVES
4

PREP TIME
10

METHOD
Sautéing

COOK TIME
20

DIRECTIONS

1. In a big skillet over medium heat, warm the olive oil. Saute the chopped onion and bell pepper for approximately five minutes or until they become tender. After adding the garlic, heat it for one more minute.

2. Add the chopped tomatoes, cumin, paprika, salt, and pepper. For ten minutes, over low heat, simmer the mixture until the tomatoes are tender and the sauce has slightly thickened.

3. Crack an egg into the four wells you made in the tomato mixture. For about five to seven minutes, or until the eggs are set to your preference, cover the skillet and cook.

4. Take off the heat and, before serving, top with optional feta cheese and chopped parsley.

INGREDIENTS

- 2 tablespoons olive oil
- 1 medium onion finely chopped.
- 1 green bell pepper seeded and diced.
- 2 cloves garlic, minced.
- 4 large tomatoes, diced.
- 1 teaspoon paprika
- 1/2 teaspoon cumin
- Salt and black pepper, to taste
- 4 large eggs
- 1/4 cup chopped fresh parsley.
- 1/4 cup crumbled feta cheese (optional)

NUTRITIONAL INFORMATION

235 calories, 12 g protein, 17 g carbohydrates, 14 g fat, 5 g fiber, 372 mg cholesterol, 408 mg sodium, 589 mg potassium.

MEDITERRANEAN EGG MUFFINS

SERVES
6

PREP TIME
15

METHOD
Baking

COOK TIME
20

DIRECTIONS

1. Turn the oven on to 375°F, or 190°C. Use muffin liners or grease a 12-cup muffin tin.

2. Combine eggs, milk, pepper, and salt in a big basin. Add the oregano, feta cheese, bell pepper, onion, and kalamata olives.

3. Evenly fill each of the muffin cups with the mixture, about 3/4 of the way.

4. Bake for about 20 minutes, or until the egg muffins are set and the tops begin to turn golden.

5. After 5 minutes of cooling, take them out of the muffin tray. Serve warm.

INGREDIENTS

- 10 large eggs
- 1/2 cup milk
- 1/2 teaspoon salt
- 1/4 teaspoon black pepper
- 1 cup chopped spinach.
- 1/2 cup diced red bell pepper.

- 1/4 cup diced red onion.
- 1/2 cup crumbled feta cheese
- 1/4 cup chopped kalamata olives.
- 1 tablespoon chopped fresh oregano.

NUTRITIONAL INFORMATION

180 calories, 12 g protein, 5 g carbohydrates, 13 g fat, 1 g fiber, 315 mg cholesterol, 410 mg sodium, 200 mg potassium.

CHAPTER 03
Snacks and Appetizers

GREEK YOGURT AND CUCUMBER DIP (TZATZIKI)

SERVES
4

PREP TIME
15

METHOD
NO-COOK

COOK TIME
0

DIRECTIONS

1. Put the grated cucumber in a sieve and squeeze out any extra water. After allowing it to drain for around five minutes, use a fresh towel or your hands to remove any leftover water.

2. Put the Greek yogurt, garlic, olive oil, fresh dill, and drained cucumber in a medium-sized bowl. Blend until all components are correctly integrated.

3. To taste, season with salt and pepper. To let the flavors merge, refrigerate for a minimum of one hour.

4. Serve chilled as a sauce for grilled meats alongside fresh veggies and pita bread.

INGREDIENTS

- 1 cup Greek yogurt
- 1 medium cucumber, peeled, seeded, and finely grated.
- 2 cloves garlic, minced.
- 2 tablespoons fresh lemon juice
- 2 tablespoons olive oil
- 2 tablespoons chopped fresh dill.
- Salt and pepper to taste

NUTRITIONAL INFORMATION

90 calories, 4 g protein, 4 g carbohydrates, 7 g fat, 0 g fiber, 5 mg cholesterol, 50 mg sodium, 120 mg potassium.

CLASSIC HUMMUS

DIRECTIONS

1. Place the tahini and lemon juice in a food processor and process for one minute. After 30 seconds of processing, scrape the bowl's bottom and sides. This additional time helps whip the tahini, producing smooth and creamy hummus.

2. To the whipped tahini and lemon juice, add the olive oil, minced garlic, cumin, and 1/2 teaspoon salt. After 30 seconds, scrape the bowl's sides and bottom, then continue processing for 30 seconds.

3. Fill the food processor with half of the chickpeas and process for one minute. Rinse the bowl's sides and bottom, add the remaining chickpeas, and process for one to two minutes or until the mixture is thick and smooth. Turn the processor on and slowly add 2 to 3 tablespoons of water until you get the right consistency if your hummus is too thick or still contains little particles of chickpea.

4. Drizzle hummus with olive oil and sprinkle with paprika. Add parsley as a garnish.

SERVES
6

PREP TIME
10

METHOD
NO-COOK

COOK TIME
0

INGREDIENTS

- 1 can (15 ounces) chickpeas, drained and rinsed.
- 1/4 cup fresh lemon juice (about 1 large lemon)
- 1/4 cup well-stirred tahini
- 1 small garlic clove, minced.
- 2 tablespoons extra virgin olive oil, plus more for serving.

- 1/2 teaspoon ground cumin
- Salt to taste
- 2 to 3 tablespoons water
- Dash of paprika, for serving
- 2 tablespoons chopped fresh parsley, for garnish.

NUTRITIONAL INFORMATION

138 calories, 4 g protein, 12 g carbohydrates, 9 g fat, 3 g fiber, 0 mg cholesterol, 200 mg sodium, 140 mg potassium.

BRUSCHETTA WITH TOMATO AND BASIL

SERVES
6

PREP TIME
15

METHOD
Baking

COOK TIME
5

DIRECTIONS

1. Set oven temperature to 400°F, or 200°C. Arrange the bread pieces onto a baking sheet and bake for approximately five minutes, or until they turn golden and crisp.

2. Add the chopped tomatoes, minced garlic, basil, olive oil, balsamic vinegar, salt, and pepper to a medium-sized bowl. Mix thoroughly by stirring.

3. Generously spoon the tomato mixture onto the slices of toasted bread.

4. Serve right away, garnishing each piece with a basil leaf.

INGREDIENTS

- 6 slices of crusty bread (like a baguette)
- 4 large ripe tomatoes finely chopped.
- 1 clove garlic, minced.
- 1/4 cup fresh basil leaves, chopped.

- 2 tablespoons extra virgin olive oil
- 1 tablespoon balsamic vinegar
- Salt and freshly ground black pepper to taste.
- Additional whole basil leaves for garnish

NUTRITIONAL INFORMATION

180 calories, 5 g protein, 27 g carbohydrates, 6 g fat, 2 g fiber, 0 mg cholesterol, 340 mg sodium, 250 mg potassium.

CAPRESE SKEWERS

SERVES
4

PREP TIME
10

METHOD
NO-COOK

COOK TIME
0

DIRECTIONS

1. Thread one mozzarella ball, one cherry tomato, and one basil leaf onto each skewer. Continue in this manner until the skewer is full. Repeat with every skewer.

2. Put the skewers in a plate arrangement. After adding a balsamic vinegar and olive oil drizzle, add salt and pepper for seasoning.

3. You may either serve right away or put it in the fridge to be served later.

INGREDIENTS

- 16 cherry tomatoes
- 16 small fresh mozzarella balls
- 16 fresh basil leaves
- 8 wooden skewers, cut in half.

- 2 tablespoons extra virgin olive oil
- 1 tablespoon balsamic vinegar
- Salt and black pepper to taste

NUTRITIONAL INFORMATION

180 calories, 12 g protein, 6 g carbohydrates, 13 g fat, 1 g fiber, 25 mg cholesterol, 200 mg sodium, 120 mg potassium.

ZUCCHINI FRITTERS

DIRECTIONS

1. After grating the zucchini, place it in a sieve, add the salt, and let it sit for ten minutes. Using paper towels or a clean dish towel, squeeze out as much moisture as you can.

2. Put the drained zucchini, flour, Parmesan, egg, garlic, and black pepper (as well as herbs) in a big bowl. Stirring is required to mix the mixture thoroughly.

3. Preheat the olive oil in a big skillet over medium-high heat. Place heaps of the zucchini mixture onto the skillet and use the back of a spoon to press them down into patties.

4. Cook until brown and crispy, about two to three minutes on each side. Transfer any extra oil to a dish covered with paper towels.

5. The final step is to serve these delicious zucchini fritters warm, with the option to serve yogurt dip or sour cream on the side. Get ready to enjoy a crispy and flavorful treat!

SERVES
4

PREP TIME
10

METHOD
Frying

COOK TIME
15

INGREDIENTS

- 2 medium zucchinis, grated.
- 1/2 teaspoon salt
- 1/4 cup all-purpose flour
- 1/4 cup grated Parmesan cheese.
- 2 cloves garlic, minced.
- 1 large egg, beaten.

- 1/2 teaspoon ground black pepper
- 2 tablespoons olive oil for frying
- Optional: 1 tablespoon fresh chopped dill or basil for extra flavor

NUTRITIONAL INFORMATION

180 calories, 6 g protein, 12 g carbohydrates, 10 g fat, 2 g fiber, 53 mg cholesterol, 340 mg sodium, 270 mg potassium.

GRILLED HALLOUMI

DIRECTIONS

1. Turn the heat to medium-high on your grill or grill pan.
2. Lightly coat the halloumi slices on both sides with olive oil, then season with black pepper and dry oregano.
3. Grill the halloumi on each side for two to three minutes or until the cheese starts melting and has grill marks.
4. Present immediately, with wedges of lemon available for squeezing over the cheese.

SERVES
4

PREP TIME
5

METHOD
Grilling

COOK TIME
10

INGREDIENTS

- 8 ounces halloumi cheese, sliced into 1/4-inch-thick pieces.
- 2 tablespoons olive oil
- 1 lemon, cut into wedges for serving.
- 1/2 teaspoon dried oregano
- Freshly ground black pepper, to taste

NUTRITIONAL INFORMATION

290 calories, 19 g protein, 2 g carbohydrates, 23 g fat, 0 g fiber, 40 mg cholesterol, 1070 mg sodium, 10 mg potassium.

MEDITERRANEAN DEVILED EGGS

SERVES
6

PREP TIME
20

METHOD
Boiling

COOK TIME
10

DIRECTIONS

1. Put the eggs in a big pot and add one inch of cold water to cover them. Over medium-high heat, bring to a boil. After that, cover, turn off the heat, and leave for ten minutes. After transferring the eggs to a bowl of ice water, let them cool fully.

2. Segment the eggs lengthwise after peeling them. The yolks should be taken out and put in a mixing dish.

3. Use a fork to mash the yolks. Add the capers, chopped olives, Dijon mustard, olive oil, lemon juice, paprika, salt, and pepper. Blend until a creamy, smooth consistency is achieved.

4. Return the yolk mixture to the egg whites by spooning or piping it. Before serving, garnish with chopped parsley.

INGREDIENTS

- 12 large eggs
- 1/4 cup mayonnaise
- 1 tablespoon Dijon mustard
- 1 tablespoon olive oil
- 1/4 cup finely chopped kalamata olives.
- 2 tablespoons capers finely chopped.
- 1 tablespoon lemon juice
- 1/4 teaspoon paprika
- Salt and pepper to taste
- 2 tablespoons chopped fresh parsley, for garnish.

NUTRITIONAL INFORMATION

180 calories, 12 g protein, 2 g carbohydrates, 14 g fat, 0 g fiber, 315 mg cholesterol, 400 mg sodium, 63 mg potassium.

TAPENADE

DIRECTIONS

1. Place Kalamata olive, capers, garlic, lemon juice, and anchovy paste in a food processor. The components should be minced finely after pulsing.

2. While the processor is operating, add the olive oil gradually and process the ingredients until it becomes a coarse paste.

3. Move the tapenade into a basin and mix in the chopped parsley and black pepper. If desired, add more pepper or lemon juice to adjust the seasoning.

4. Serve immediately with crusty bread or store in the refrigerator for up to a week in an airtight container.

SERVES
4

PREP TIME
10

METHOD
NO-COOK

COOK TIME
0

INGREDIENTS

- 1 cup pitted Kalamata olive
- 2 cloves garlic, minced.
- 2 tablespoons capers rinsed and drained.
- 1 tablespoon fresh lemon juice
- 2 teaspoons anchovy paste (optional)
- 1/3 cup extra virgin olive oil
- 1/4 teaspoon freshly ground black pepper.
- 2 tablespoons chopped fresh parsley.

NUTRITIONAL INFORMATION

190 calories, 1 g protein, 4 g carbohydrates, 19 g fat, 2 g fiber, 2 mg cholesterol, 610 mg sodium, 10 mg potassium.

MUSHROOM AND GOAT CHEESE CROSTINI

SERVES
6

PREP TIME
15

METHOD
Topping and
Baking

COOK TIME
10

DIRECTIONS

1. Turn the oven on to 375°F, or 190°C. Place the baguette pieces in an arrangement on a baking sheet and lightly coat with olive oil—toast for approximately five minutes, or until lightly browned.

2. In a large skillet, heat the remaining olive oil over medium heat. After 30 seconds of sautéing the garlic, add the mushrooms, salt, and pepper. Simmer for 5 to 7 minutes or until the mushrooms are soft and the liquid has evaporated.

3. Top each toasted baguette slice with a dollop of goat cheese and the sautéed mushrooms. Sprinkle with fresh thyme.

4. Put the crostini back in the oven and let it bake for a further five minutes, or until the goat cheese has melted somewhat. Drizzle with balsamic glaze prior to serving, if desired.

INGREDIENTS

- 1 baguette, sliced into 1/2-inch-thick pieces.
- 2 tablespoons olive oil
- 1 pound cremini mushrooms thinly sliced.
- 2 cloves garlic, minced.
- 1/4 teaspoon salt
- 1/4 teaspoon black pepper
- 1/2 cup goat cheese, softened.
- 2 tablespoons fresh thyme leaves
- Balsamic glaze for drizzling (optional)

NUTRITIONAL INFORMATION

220 calories, 9 g protein, 24 g carbohydrates, 10 g fat, 2 g fiber, 13 mg cholesterol, 350 mg sodium, 240 mg potassium.

ROASTED RED PEPPER HUMMUS

DIRECTIONS

1. Place the chickpeas, garlic, tahini, roasted red pepper, lemon juice, olive oil, cumin, salt, and pepper in a food processor and process until smooth.

2. Add water to the hummus one tablespoon at a time while the machine operates until the desired consistency is reached.

3. Taste and adjust the seasoning to your liking. Before serving, if wanted, add some chopped parsley and a little more olive oil as garnish.

SERVES
6

PREP TIME
10

METHOD
NO-COOK

COOK TIME
0

INGREDIENTS

- 1 (15 oz) can chickpeas, drained and rinsed
- 1 large roasted red pepper (about 1/2 cup, chopped)
- 2 tablespoons tahini
- 2 cloves garlic, minced.
- Juice of 1 lemon
- 2 tablespoons olive oil
- 1/2 teaspoon ground cumin
- Salt and pepper to taste
- 2 tablespoons water, or as needed.
- Optional garnish: chopped parsley and a drizzle of olive oil

NUTRITIONAL INFORMATION

140 calories, 5 g protein, 16 g carbohydrates, 7 g fat, 4 g fiber, 0 mg cholesterol, 240 mg sodium, 210 mg potassium.

PISTACHIO AND POMEGRANATE MUHAMMARA

DIRECTIONS

1. Put the breadcrumbs, pomegranate molasses, roasted red peppers, pistachios, cumin, garlic, and red pepper flakes in a food processor. Process until thoroughly combined.

2. Slowly trickle in the olive oil while the processor operates to achieve a smooth and creamy mixture. Add salt to taste to season.

3. To allow the flavors to mingle, move the muhammara to a serving dish and place it in the refrigerator for at least half an hour.

4. Add chopped parsley and pomegranate seeds as a garnish before serving.

SERVES
4

PREP TIME
15

METHOD
NO-COOK

COOK TIME
0

INGREDIENTS

- 1 cup roasted red peppers, drained and chopped.
- 1/2 cup shelled pistachios.
- 1/3 cup breadcrumbs
- 2 tablespoons pomegranate molasses
- 1 clove garlic, minced.
- 1 teaspoon ground cumin
- 1/2 teaspoon crushed red pepper flakes.
- 1/4 cup olive oil
- Salt to taste
- 1/4 cup pomegranate seeds (for garnish)
- 2 tablespoons chopped fresh parsley (for garnish)

NUTRITIONAL INFORMATION

290 calories, 6 g protein, 18 g carbohydrates, 22 g fat, 3 g fiber, 0 mg cholesterol, 300 mg sodium, 350 mg potassium.

SMOKED SALMON AND CREAM CHEESE ROLLS

SERVES
4

PREP TIME
15

METHOD
NO-COOK

COOK TIME
0

DIRECTIONS

1. To make the cream cheese spreadable, combine the lemon zest, capers, dill, and lemon juice in a small bowl.
2. Lay out the tortillas and, leaving a thin border around the borders, evenly spread the cream cheese mixture over each one.
3. Spread the slices of smoked salmon in a single layer on top of the cream cheese.
4. Tightly roll the tortillas, cover them with plastic wrap, and refrigerate them for at least half an hour to solidify.
5. Cut each roll into 1-inch portions when ready to serve by removing the plastic wrap.

INGREDIENTS

- 8 oz smoked salmon thinly sliced.
- 4 oz cream cheese, softened.
- 1 tablespoon fresh dill, chopped.
- 1 tablespoon capers, drained and chopped.
- 1 teaspoon lemon zest
- 1 tablespoon lemon juice
- 4 large whole wheat tortillas

NUTRITIONAL INFORMATION

280 calories, 18 g protein, 22 g carbohydrates, 15 g fat, 3 g fiber, 30 mg cholesterol, 910 mg sodium, 200 mg potassium.

CHAPTER 04
Salads

GREEK VILLAGE SALAD (HORIATIKI)

DIRECTIONS

1. Place the bell pepper, red onion, cucumber slices, and tomato wedges in a big salad bowl.
2. Include the Kalamata olives and place feta cheese slices on top. Evenly distribute the dry oregano over the salad.
3. Drizzle with red wine vinegar and olive oil. To taste, add salt and pepper for seasoning.
4. Without shattering the feta cheese, gently toss the salad to combine the ingredients. Serve right away.

SERVES
4

PREP TIME
20

METHOD
NO-COOK

COOK TIME
0

INGREDIENTS

- 3 medium ripe tomatoes, cut into wedges.
- 1 cucumber, sliced into thick half-moons.
- 1 small red onion thinly sliced.
- 1 bell pepper (green or red), sliced.
- 1/2 cup Kalamata olives, pitted.
- 6 ounces feta cheese, cut into thick slices.
- 1 teaspoon dried oregano
- 3 tablespoons extra virgin olive oil
- 2 tablespoons red wine vinegar
- Salt and freshly ground black pepper to taste.

NUTRITIONAL INFORMATION

250 calories, 7 g protein, 14 g carbohydrates, 19 g fat, 3 g fiber, 25 mg cholesterol, 560 mg sodium, 350 mg potassium.

TABBOULEH

DIRECTIONS

1. Place the bulgur wheat and the boiling water in a big basin. Once the bulgur is soft and the water has been absorbed, cover and let it sit for fifteen minutes. Using a fork, fluff.

2. Top the bulgur with chopped tomatoes, cucumber, red onion, mint, and parsley.

3. Combine the lemon juice, olive oil, salt, and pepper in a small bowl. Drizzle the bulgur mixture on top, then mix thoroughly.

4. Taste and adjust the seasoning before serving cold or at room temperature.

SERVES
4

PREP TIME
20

METHOD
NO-COOK

COOK TIME
0

INGREDIENTS

- 1 cup bulgur wheat
- 1 cup boiling water.
- 2 cups finely chopped fresh parsley.
- 1/2 cup finely chopped fresh mint.
- 2 medium tomatoes, diced.
- 1 small cucumber, diced.
- 1/4 cup finely chopped red onion.
- 1/4 cup fresh lemon juice
- 1/4 cup extra virgin olive oil
- Salt and freshly ground black pepper to taste.

NUTRITIONAL INFORMATION

180 calories, 4 g protein, 24 g carbohydrates, 8 g fat, 5 g fiber, 0 mg cholesterol, 120 mg sodium, 350 mg potassium.

WATERMELON AND FETA SALAD

DIRECTIONS

1. Combine the chopped mint leaves, thinly sliced red onion, crumbled feta cheese, and cubed watermelon in a big bowl.
2. Combine the lime juice, extra virgin olive oil, salt, and pepper in a small bowl.
3. Pour the dressing over the watermelon mixture and mix it with a gentle toss.
4. To enable the flavors to mingle, serve immediately or chill in the refrigerator for ten to fifteen minutes.

SERVES
4

PREP TIME
10

METHOD
NO-COOK

COOK TIME
0

INGREDIENTS

- 4 cups watermelon, cubed.
- 1/2 cup feta cheese, crumbled.
- 1/4 cup fresh mint leaves, chopped.
- 1/4 small red onion thinly sliced.

- 2 tablespoons extra virgin olive oil
- 1 tablespoon lime juice
- Salt and freshly ground black pepper to taste.

NUTRITIONAL INFORMATION

150 calories, 4 g protein, 15 g carbohydrates, 9 g fat, 1 g fiber, 15 mg cholesterol, 240 mg sodium, 200 mg potassium.

CHICKPEA AND SPINACH SALAD

DIRECTIONS

1. Combine the feta cheese, chopped parsley, cherry tomatoes, red onion, chickpeas, and baby spinach in a large salad dish.
2. Combine the olive oil, lemon juice, Dijon mustard, salt, and pepper in a small bowl.
3. Drizzle the salad with the dressing and gently toss to mix.
4. You can serve it immediately or let it cool in the fridge for up to half an hour before serving

SERVES
4

PREP TIME
15

METHOD
NO-COOK

COOK TIME
0

INGREDIENTS

- 2 cups fresh baby spinach
- 1 can (15 ounces) chickpeas, drained and rinsed.
- 1 cup cherry tomatoes, halved.
- 1/4 red onion thinly sliced.
- 1/4 cup crumbled feta cheese
- 1/4 cup chopped fresh parsley.
- 2 tablespoons extra virgin olive oil
- 1 tablespoon lemon juice
- 1 teaspoon Dijon mustard
- Salt and freshly ground black pepper to taste.

NUTRITIONAL INFORMATION

210 calories, 8 g protein, 23 g carbohydrates, 10 g fat, 6 g fiber, 10 mg cholesterol, 390 mg sodium, 420 mg potassium.

MEDITERRANEAN BEET SALAD

SERVES
4

PREP TIME
15

METHOD
Roasting

COOK TIME
40

DIRECTIONS

1.Set the oven's temperature to 400°F. Place every beet on a baking sheet after wrapping it in aluminum foil. Bake for forty minutes or until the vegetable is soft. After letting cool, peel and chop into small pieces.

2. Combine the olive oil, honey, red wine vinegar, salt, and black pepper in a small bowl.

3. Combine the feta cheese crumbles, chopped parsley, toasted walnuts, and roasted beets in a big bowl.

4. Drizzle the salad with the dressing and gently toss to mix. Serve right away.

INGREDIENTS

- 4 medium beets trimmed and scrubbed.
- 2 tablespoons extra virgin olive oil
- 2 tablespoons red wine vinegar
- 1 teaspoon honey
- 1/2 teaspoon salt
- 1/4 teaspoon black pepper
- 1/4 cup crumbled feta cheese
- 1/4 cup chopped fresh parsley.
- 1/4 cup chopped walnuts, toasted.

NUTRITIONAL INFORMATION

210 calories, 5 g protein, 20 g carbohydrates, 13 g fat, 4 g fiber, 10 mg cholesterol, 310 mg sodium, 400 mg potassium.

CUCUMBER AND YOGURT SALAD (CACIK)

DIRECTIONS

1. Greek yogurt, finely diced cucumbers, minced garlic, olive oil, fresh mint, fresh dill, and lemon juice should all be combined in a big bowl.

2. Thoroughly stir until all components are dispersed equally. To taste, add salt and pepper for seasoning.

3. To allow the flavors to mingle, chill in the refrigerator for at least ten minutes before serving.

4. Optional: Before serving, sprinkle some paprika and dried mint over top.

SERVES
4

PREP TIME
15

METHOD
NO-COOK

COOK TIME
0

INGREDIENTS

- 2 cups plain Greek yogurt
- 2 medium cucumbers, peeled, seeded, and finely chopped.
- 2 cloves garlic, minced.
- 2 tablespoons olive oil
- 1 tablespoon fresh dill, chopped.
- 1 tablespoon fresh mint, chopped.
- 1 tablespoon lemon juice
- Salt and freshly ground black pepper to taste.
- 1/2 teaspoon dried mint (optional)
- 1/2 teaspoon paprika (optional)

NUTRITIONAL INFORMATION

120 calories, 5 g protein, 8 g carbohydrates, 7 g fat, 1 g fiber, 10 mg cholesterol, 100 mg sodium, 200 mg potassium.

ROASTED PEPPER AND ARTICHOKE SALAD

DIRECTIONS

1. Set the oven's temperature to 425°F. After placing the bell peppers on a baking sheet, roast them for 20 minutes, rotating them halfway through until the skins are blistered and browned. Take it out of the oven and put it in a plastic bag that is sealed to steam for ten minutes. After peeling, cut into strips.

2. Place the quartered artichoke hearts and the roasted pepper strips in a big salad dish.

3. Combine the olive oil, balsamic vinegar, salt, pepper, and dried oregano in a small bowl. Drizzle the salad with the dressing and toss to coat.

4. Before serving, toss the salad with chopped fresh parsley and crumbled feta cheese.

SERVES
4

PREP TIME
15

METHOD
Roasting

COOK TIME
20

INGREDIENTS

- 2 red bell peppers
- 2 yellow bell peppers
- 1 (14-ounce) can artichoke hearts, drained and quartered
- 1/4 cup extra virgin olive oil
- 2 tablespoons balsamic vinegar
- 1 teaspoon dried oregano
- Salt and freshly ground black pepper to taste.
- 1/4 cup crumbled feta cheese
- 2 tablespoons chopped fresh parsley.

NUTRITIONAL INFORMATION

180 calories, 3 g protein, 13 g carbohydrates, 14 g fat, 5 g fiber, 8 mg cholesterol, 420 mg sodium, 310 mg potassium.

FIG AND ARUGULA SALAD

DIRECTIONS

1. Put the arugula in a big salad dish and sprinkle the quartered figs on top.
2. Top the arugula and figs with a scattering of toasted walnuts and crumbled goat cheese.
3. Drizzle extra virgin olive oil and balsamic glaze over the salad.
4. Toss with freshly ground black pepper and salt to taste. After gently tossing to mix, serve right away.

SERVES
4

PREP TIME
10

METHOD
NO-COOK

COOK TIME
0

INGREDIENTS

- 6 cups arugula
- 8 fresh figs, quartered.
- 1/4 cup crumbled goat cheese
- 1/4 cup toasted walnuts, chopped.
- 2 tablespoons balsamic glaze
- 2 tablespoons extra virgin olive oil
- Salt and freshly ground black pepper to taste.

NUTRITIONAL INFORMATION

210 calories, 5 g protein, 21 g carbohydrates, 13 g fat, 5 g fiber, 5 mg cholesterol, 150 mg sodium, 350 mg potassium.

MEDITERRANEAN CAULIFLOWER SALAD

SERVES
4

PREP TIME
15

METHOD
Blanching

COOK TIME
5

DIRECTIONS

1. Fill a big saucepan with boiling salted water. When the cauliflower florets are soft but still crisp, add them and simmer for three to four minutes. To cease cooking, drain and rinse with cold water.
2. Put the cooked cauliflower, parsley, cherry tomatoes, red onion, and Kalamata olives in a big bowl.
3. Combine the olive oil, lemon juice, salt, pepper, and dried oregano in a small bowl. Drizzle the salad with the dressing and toss to coat.
4. Before serving, sprinkle some crumbled feta cheese over the salad.

INGREDIENTS

- 1 medium head cauliflower, cut into small florets.
- 1/2 cup cherry tomatoes, halved.
- 1/4 cup red onion finely chopped.
- 1/4 cup Kalamata olives pitted and halved.
- 1/4 cup fresh parsley, chopped.
- 1/4 cup feta cheese, crumbled.
- 3 tablespoons extra virgin olive oil
- 2 tablespoons lemon juice
- 1 teaspoon dried oregano
- Salt and freshly ground black pepper to taste.

NUTRITIONAL INFORMATION

180 calories, 5 g protein, 13 g carbohydrates, 14 g fat, 5 g fiber, 15 mg cholesterol, 400 mg sodium, 450 mg potassium.

AVOCADO AND QUINOA SALAD

DIRECTIONS

1. Rinse the quinoa well in cold water. Heat the water and salt in a medium pot until they boil. After adding the quinoa, turn down the heat to low, cover, and simmer until the water is absorbed, about 15 minutes. Use a fork and fluff, and allow it to cool.
2. Put the chilled quinoa, chopped avocado, cherry tomatoes, red onion, and cilantro in a big bowl.
3. Combine the lime juice, olive oil, salt, and pepper in a small bowl. After adding the dressing to the quinoa mixture, gently toss to mix.
4. To let the flavors mingle, serve right away or chill for up to two hours.

SERVES
4

PREP TIME
15

METHOD
Boiling

COOK TIME
15

INGREDIENTS

- 1 cup quinoa
- 2 cups water
- 1/2 teaspoon salt
- 1 large avocado, diced.
- 1 cup cherry tomatoes, halved.
- 1 small red onion finely chopped.
- 1/4 cup fresh cilantro, chopped.
- 2 tablespoons lime juice
- 3 tablespoons olive oil
- Salt and freshly ground black pepper to taste.

NUTRITIONAL INFORMATION

320 calories, 6 g protein, 30 g carbohydrates, 21 g fat, 7 g fiber, 0 mg cholesterol, 170 mg sodium, 540 mg potassium

BROCCOLI AND CHICKPEA SALAD

DIRECTIONS

1. Start by boiling some water in a kettle. When the broccoli florets are crisp-tender, add them and simmer for three minutes. To cease cooking, drain and rinse with cold water.

2. Combine the broccoli, dried cranberries, sunflower seeds, red onion, chickpeas, and crumbled feta cheese in [a large mixing bowl].

3. Combine the olive oil, Dijon mustard, lemon juice, and red wine vinegar in a small bowl. To taste, add salt and pepper for seasoning.

4. Drizzle the salad with the dressing and toss to mix. Serve immediately or refrigerate until ready to serve.

SERVES
4

PREP TIME
15

METHOD
Boiling

COOK TIME
5

INGREDIENTS

- 1 head broccoli, cut into small florets.
- 1 can (15 ounces) chickpeas, drained and rinsed.
- 1/2 red onion finely chopped.
- 1/4 cup sunflower seeds
- 1/4 cup dried cranberries
- 1/4 cup crumbled feta cheese

- 3 tablespoons olive oil
- 2 tablespoons lemon juice
- 1 tablespoon red wine vinegar
- 1 teaspoon Dijon mustard
- Salt and freshly ground black pepper to taste.

NUTRITIONAL INFORMATION

220 calories, 7 g protein, 25 g carbohydrates, 11 g fat, 7 g fiber, 10 mg cholesterol, 320 mg sodium, 400 mg potassium.

GRILLED CALAMARI SALAD

SERVES
4

PREP TIME
10

METHOD
Grilling

COOK TIME
20

DIRECTIONS

1. Turn the grill to medium-high. Toss the calamari rings in a basin with olive oil, oregano, lemon juice, minced garlic, salt, and pepper.

2. Grill the calamari until it's barely cooked through and has a light sear on both sides, about 2 to 3 minutes per side. Remove it from the grill and place it aside.

3. Combine the mixed salad greens, chopped parsley, cherry tomatoes, red onion, and Kalamata olives in a large salad bowl.

4. Gently toss the salad with the grilled calamari after adding it. Serve right away.

INGREDIENTS

- 1-pound calamari, cleaned and cut into rings
- 2 tablespoons olive oil
- 2 cloves garlic, minced.
- 1 lemon, juiced.
- 1 teaspoon dried oregano
- Salt and freshly ground black pepper to taste.

- 4 cups mixed salad greens
- 1 cup cherry tomatoes, halved.
- 1/2 cup red onion thinly sliced.
- 1/4 cup Kalamata olives pitted and halved.
- 1/4 cup fresh parsley, chopped.

NUTRITIONAL INFORMATION

180 calories, 18 g protein, 8 g carbohydrates, 8 g fat, 2 g fiber, 220 mg cholesterol, 450 mg sodium, 420 mg potassium.

CHAPTER 05
Soups

CLASSIC MINESTRONE SOUP

SERVES
6

PREP TIME
20

METHOD
Simmering

COOK TIME
40

DIRECTIONS

1. Heat olive oil in a large pot over medium heat. Add the diced onion, garlic, carrots, and celery. Cook until the vegetables are tender, about 10 minutes.
2. Stir in the zucchini, yellow squash, diced tomatoes (with juice), and vegetable broth. Bring to a boil, then reduce heat and simmer for 20 minutes.
3. Add the cannellini beans, small pasta, dried oregano, and dried basil. Simmer for an additional 10 minutes, or until the pasta is cooked.
4. Stir in the chopped spinach and cook until wilted, about 2 minutes. Season with salt and pepper to taste.
5. Serve hot, topped with grated Parmesan cheese if desired.

INGREDIENTS

- 2 tablespoons olive oil
- 1 medium onion, diced.
- 2 cloves garlic, minced.
- 2 carrots peeled and diced.
- 2 celery stalks, diced.
- 1 zucchini, diced.
- 1 yellow squash, diced.
- 1 (14.5-ounce) can diced tomatoes
- 6 cups vegetable broth
- 1 (15-ounce) can cannellini beans, drained and rinsed
- 1 cup small pasta (like ditalini or elbow)
- 2 cups chopped fresh spinach.
- 1 teaspoon dried oregano
- 1 teaspoon dried basil
- Salt and pepper to taste
- Grated Parmesan cheese, for serving

NUTRITIONAL INFORMATION

210 calories, 8 g protein, 35 g carbohydrates, 5 g fat, 6 g fiber, 0 mg cholesterol, 720 mg sodium, 470 mg potassium.

LENTIL AND SPINACH SOUP

SERVES
4

PREP TIME
10

METHOD
Simmering

COOK TIME
25

DIRECTIONS

1. Heat the olive oil in a big pot over medium heat. Cook the chopped onion, carrots, and celery for approximately five minutes or until tender. One more minute is spent cooking after adding the minced garlic.

2. Add the diced tomatoes with juice, vegetable broth, bay leaf, ground cumin, and dry thyme. Once the lentils are soft, boil, lower the heat, and simmer for 25 minutes.

3. Take out the bay leaf and add the chopped spinach after stirring. Cook the spinach for a further two minutes or until it wilts. To taste, add salt and pepper for seasoning.

INGREDIENTS

- 1 cup dried lentils, rinsed.
- 6 cups vegetable broth
- 1 medium onion, chopped.
- 2 carrots, diced.
- 2 celery stalks, diced.
- 3 cloves garlic, minced.
- 1 (14.5 oz) can diced tomatoes

- 1 teaspoon ground cumin
- 1 teaspoon dried thyme
- 1 bay leaf
- 4 cups fresh spinach, chopped.
- 2 tablespoons olive oil
- Salt and pepper to taste

NUTRITIONAL INFORMATION

220 calories, 12 g protein, 32 g carbohydrates, 6 g fat, 10 g fiber, 0 mg cholesterol, 520 mg sodium, 450 mg potassium.

GREEK LEMON CHICKEN SOUP (AVGOLEMONO)

DIRECTIONS

1. Bring the chicken stock to a boil in a large pot. After adding the rice, lower the heat to medium and cook for about 20 minutes or until the rice is cooked.
2. In a medium-sized bowl, thoroughly mix the eggs and lemon juice.
3. To temper the eggs, gradually pour about a cup of hot broth into the egg and lemon mixture while whisking constantly.
4. Stir the egg mixture that has been tempered gradually back into the pot containing the rice and stock. Don't let the soup boil; add the shredded chicken and heat through.
5. Toss with freshly ground black pepper and salt to taste. If desired, garnish with freshly chopped dill. Serve right away.

SERVES
4

PREP TIME
15

METHOD
Simmering

COOK TIME
30

INGREDIENTS

- 6 cups chicken broth
- 1/2 cup uncooked white rice
- 3 large eggs
- 1/3 cup fresh lemon juice (about 2 lemons)

- 2 cups cooked chicken breast, shredded.
- Salt and freshly ground black pepper to taste.
- 2 tablespoons fresh chopped dill (optional)

NUTRITIONAL INFORMATION

250 calories, 20 g protein, 20 g carbohydrates, 9 g fat, 1 g fiber, 140 mg cholesterol, 850 mg sodium, 280 mg potassium.

MEDITERRANEAN VEGETABLE SOUP

DIRECTIONS

1. In a large pot over medium heat, warm the olive oil. Add the onion and garlic, and cook for about 5 minutes or until the onion becomes transparent.

2. Include the red bell pepper, yellow bell pepper, zucchini, carrots, and celery. Cook for five minutes, stirring from time to time.

3. Add the diced tomatoes, salt, pepper, oregano, basil, thyme, and vegetable broth. Bring to a boil, then simmer for 20 minutes on low heat.

4. Include the lemon juice, parsley, and fresh spinach. Simmer for five more minutes. Warm up the food.

SERVES
4

PREP TIME
15

METHOD
Simmering

COOK TIME
30

INGREDIENTS

- 2 tablespoons olive oil
- 1 large onion, chopped.
- 2 garlic cloves, minced.
- 2 medium carrots, chopped.
- 2 celery stalks, chopped.
- 1 medium zucchini, chopped.
- 1 red bell pepper, chopped.
- 1 yellow bell pepper, chopped.
- 1 can (14.5 ounces) diced tomatoes.

- 4 cups vegetable broth
- 1 teaspoon dried oregano
- 1 teaspoon dried basil
- 1/2 teaspoon dried thyme
- Salt and pepper to taste
- 1 cup chopped fresh spinach.
- 1/4 cup chopped fresh parsley.
- Juice of 1 lemon

NUTRITIONAL INFORMATION

160 calories, 4 g protein, 22 g carbohydrates, 7 g fat, 5 g fiber, 0 mg cholesterol, 640 mg sodium, 600 mg potassium.

CHICKPEA AND TOMATO SOUP

SERVES
4

PREP TIME
10

METHOD
Simmering

COOK TIME
30

DIRECTIONS

1. Warm the olive oil in a large pot over medium heat. Add the chopped onion and simmer for about 5 minutes or until softened. Cook for an additional minute after adding the smoked paprika, ground cumin, and minced garlic.

2. Fill the pot with the chickpeas, diced tomatoes (including juice), and vegetable broth. After bringing to a boil, lower the heat and simmer for twenty minutes.

3. Season to taste with salt and pepper. Transfer half of the soup to a blender, blend until smooth, and then return to the pot. Alternatively, use an immersion blender to puree the soup to your preferred consistency partially.

4. If using, stir in the freshly cut parsley and serve hot.

INGREDIENTS

- 2 tablespoons olive oil
- 1 medium onion, chopped.
- 2 cloves garlic, minced.
- 1 teaspoon ground cumin
- 1 teaspoon smoked paprika.
- 1 (15-ounce) can chickpeas, drained and rinsed

- 1 (28-ounce) can diced tomatoes
- 4 cups vegetable broth
- Salt and freshly ground black pepper to taste.
- 1/4 cup fresh parsley, chopped (optional)

NUTRITIONAL INFORMATION

180 calories, 6 g protein, 28 g carbohydrates, 5 g fat, 7 g fiber, 0 mg cholesterol, 700 mg sodium, 450 mg potassium.

TUSCAN WHITE BEAN SOUP

SERVES
4

PREP TIME
15

METHOD
Simmering

COOK TIME
30

DIRECTIONS

1. Warm the olive oil in a large pot over medium heat. Stir in the chopped celery, carrots, and onion. Simmer for about ten minutes or until the veggies are soft, stirring occasionally.
2. Cook the minced garlic for another one to two minutes or until it turns golden brown and becomes aromatic.
3. Add the bay leaf, dried thyme, rosemary, diced tomatoes, and [canned] cannellini beans to the vegetable broth. After bringing to a boil, lower the heat and simmer for fifteen minutes.
4. After adding the chopped kale, boil it for five more minutes or until it becomes soft. To taste, add salt and pepper for seasoning. Remove the bay leaf before serving.
5. If preferred, top the hot dish with grated Parmesan cheese.

INGREDIENTS

- 2 tablespoons olive oil
- 1 medium onion, chopped.
- 2 carrots, chopped.
- 2 celery stalks, chopped.
- 4 cloves garlic, minced.
- 4 cups vegetable broth
- 2 cans (15 ounces each) cannellini beans, drained and rinsed.
- 1 can (14.5 ounces) diced tomatoes.

- 1 teaspoon dried rosemary
- 1 teaspoon dried thyme
- 1 bay leaf
- 2 cups chopped kale.
- Salt and freshly ground black pepper to taste.
- 1/4 cup grated Parmesan cheese (optional)

NUTRITIONAL INFORMATION

240 calories, 10 g protein, 38 g carbohydrates, 6 g fat, 10 g fiber, 0 mg cholesterol, 600 mg sodium, 500 mg potassium.

ROASTED RED PEPPER AND TOMATO SOUP

SERVES
4

PREP TIME
15

METHOD
Roasting-
Simmering

COOK TIME
45

DIRECTIONS

1. Preheat the oven to 425°F. Arrange the tomatoes, garlic, onion, and red bell peppers on a baking sheet. Apply a light coating of olive oil and roast the veggies for half an hour or until they become soft and have a hint of browning.

2. Remove the roasted veggies from the oven and let them cool a bit. Remove the peel from the tomatoes and red bell peppers.

3. Pour the roasted veggies into a big pot. Stir in the dried thyme, dry basil, and vegetable broth. After bringing to a boil, lower the heat and simmer for fifteen minutes.

4. Puree the soup with an immersion blender until smooth. Season with salt and pepper to taste. Serve warm.

INGREDIENTS

- 4 large red bell peppers
- 4 large tomatoes, halved.
- 1 medium onion, quartered.
- 4 cloves garlic, peeled.

- 3 tablespoons olive oil
- 4 cups vegetable broth
- 1 teaspoon dried basil
- 1/2 teaspoon dried thyme
- Salt and pepper to taste

NUTRITIONAL INFORMATION

140 calories, 3 g protein, 20 g carbohydrates, 7 g fat, 4 g fiber, 0 mg cholesterol, 600 mg sodium, 500 mg potassium.

MEDITERRANEAN FISH SOUP

SERVES
4

PREP TIME
15

METHOD
Sautéing-
Simmering

COOK TIME
30

DIRECTIONS

1. Warm the olive oil in a big pot over medium heat. Add the chopped red bell pepper, celery, carrots, onion, and garlic. Sauté for ten minutes or until the veggies are tender.
2. Add the fish stock or vegetable broth, diced tomatoes, and their juice. Bring to a boil, then lower the heat and simmer for fifteen minutes.
3. Add the basil, thyme, parsley, and fish pieces. Simmer for 10 minutes or until the fish is cooked and readily flakes with a fork. To taste, add salt and pepper for seasoning.
4. Present the soup hot, with lemon wedges on the side as a garnish. Serve warm.

INGREDIENTS

- 2 tablespoons olive oil
- 1 medium onion, chopped.
- 2 cloves garlic, minced.
- 2 celery stalks, chopped.
- 2 carrots, chopped.
- 1 red bell pepper, chopped.
- 1 (14.5-ounce) can diced tomatoes

- 4 cups fish stock or vegetable broth
- 1-pound white fish fillets (such as cod or halibut), cut into bite-sized pieces
- 1/2 cup chopped fresh parsley.
- 1 teaspoon dried thyme
- 1 teaspoon dried basil

NUTRITIONAL INFORMATION

220 calories, 20 g protein, 18 g carbohydrates, 8 g fat, 3 g fiber, 45 mg cholesterol, 700 mg sodium, 450 mg potassium.

SPICY MOROCCAN LENTIL SOUP

DIRECTIONS

1. Warm the olive oil in a big pot over medium heat. Add the chopped onion and simmer for about 5 minutes or until softened. Cook for an additional five minutes after adding the diced carrots and minced garlic.
2. After adding the ground cumin, coriander, cinnamon, and cayenne pepper, cook for 1 minute or until aromatic.
3. Include the tomato paste, diced tomatoes, lentils, and vegetable broth. After bringing to a boil, lower the heat and simmer the lentils for 30 minutes or until soft.
4. As the lentils simmer to perfection, season with a sprinkle of black pepper and salt. The addition of lemon juice and chopped cilantro will add a refreshing twist. Serve this comforting bowl of goodness hot, and let it warm your soul.

SERVES
4

PREP TIME
15

METHOD
Simmering

COOK TIME
45

INGREDIENTS

- 2 tablespoons olive oil
- 1 large onion, chopped.
- 3 cloves garlic, minced.
- 2 large carrots, diced.
- 1 teaspoon ground cumin
- 1 teaspoon ground coriander
- 1/2 teaspoon ground cinnamon
- 1/4 teaspoon cayenne pepper

- 1 cup dried green lentils, rinsed.
- 6 cups vegetable broth
- 1 can (14.5 ounces) diced tomatoes.
- 1/4 cup tomato paste
- 1/2 teaspoon salt
- 1/4 teaspoon black pepper
- 1/4 cup chopped fresh cilantro.
- Juice of 1 lemon

NUTRITIONAL INFORMATION

280 calories, 13 g protein, 45 g carbohydrates, 6 g fat, 14 g fiber, 0 mg cholesterol, 870 mg sodium, 780 mg potassium.

CREAMY CAULIFLOWER AND GARLIC SOUP

SERVES
4

PREP TIME
15

METHOD
Simmering

COOK TIME
30

DIRECTIONS

1. Heat the olive oil in a big pot over medium heat. Add the minced garlic, chopped onion, and sauté for about 5 minutes, or until the ingredients are soft and fragrant.
2. Include the vegetable broth and the cauliflower florets. After bringing to a boil, lower the heat and simmer for 20 minutes or until the cauliflower is soft.
3. Puree the soup with an immersion blender until it's smooth. Another option is to transfer the soup to a blender carefully, process it until it's soft, and then pour it back into the pot.
4. Add the heavy cream and taste-test to adjust for salt and pepper. Continue to heat through for five more minutes, careful not to let it boil.
5. If preferred, top a hot dish with fresh parsley.

INGREDIENTS

- 1 large head cauliflower, cut into florets.
- 1 large onion, chopped.
- 4 cloves garlic, minced.
- 4 cups vegetable broth
- 1 cup heavy cream
- 2 tablespoons olive oil
- Salt and freshly ground black pepper to taste.
- Fresh parsley for garnish (optional)

NUTRITIONAL INFORMATION

230 calories, 5 g protein, 18 g carbohydrates, 16 g fat, 4 g fiber, 45 mg cholesterol, 500 mg sodium, 350 mg potassium.

SPANISH GAZPACHO

SERVES
4

PREP TIME
20

METHOD
No-Cook

COOK TIME
0

DIRECTIONS

1. Put the diced tomatoes, cucumber, red onion, bell pepper, and garlic in a blender and process until smooth.
2. Fill the blender with the red wine vinegar, olive oil, salt, black pepper, and cold water. Blend one more until smooth and fully integrated.
3. Taste and correct the seasoning if needed. Before serving, let the gazpacho cool in the fridge for at least one hour.
4. If desired, top with freshly chopped basil and serve chilled.

INGREDIENTS

- 2 pounds ripe tomatoes cored and roughly chopped.
- 1 cucumber peeled and roughly chopped.
- 1 small red bell pepper seeded and roughly chopped.
- 1 small red onion roughly chopped.
- 2 cloves garlic, peeled.
- 3 tablespoons red wine vinegar
- 1/4 cup extra virgin olive oil
- 1 teaspoon salt
- 1/2 teaspoon freshly ground black pepper.
- 1 cup cold water

NUTRITIONAL INFORMATION

180 calories, 3 g protein, 18 g carbohydrates, 12 g fat, 4 g fiber, 0 mg cholesterol, 610 mg sodium, 550 mg potassium.

HEARTY BARLEY AND MUSHROOM SOUP

DIRECTIONS

1. Heat the olive oil in a big pot over medium heat. Add the chopped onion and garlic, and cook for about 5 minutes or until the onion becomes transparent.

2. Include the freshly sliced mushrooms, celery, and cubed carrots. Cook until the vegetables start to soften, about five more minutes.

3. Add the bay leaf, dried thyme, pearl barley, and vegetable broth. After bringing to a boil, lower the heat and simmer the barley for thirty-five minutes, or until it becomes soft.

4. Toss with freshly ground black pepper and salt to taste. Take out the bay leaf, add the parsley that has been chopped, and serve hot.

SERVES
4

PREP TIME
15

METHOD
Simmering

COOK TIME
45

INGREDIENTS

- ·1 tablespoon olive oil
- ·1 medium onion, diced.
- ·2 cloves garlic, minced.
- ·2 medium carrots, diced.
- ·2 celery stalks, diced.
- ·8 ounces cremini mushrooms, sliced.
- ·1 cup pearl barley

- ·6 cups vegetable broth
- ·1 teaspoon dried thyme
- ·1 bay leaf
- ·Salt and freshly ground black pepper to taste.
- ·2 tablespoons fresh parsley, chopped.

NUTRITIONAL INFORMATION

230 calories, 6 g protein, 41 g carbohydrates, 5 g fat, 8 g fiber, 0 mg cholesterol, 700 mg sodium, 400 mg potassium.

CHAPTER 06
Fish and Seafood

GRILLED SALMON WITH LEMON AND DILL

DIRECTIONS

1. Turn the heat up to medium-high.
2. Brush the salmon fillets on both sides with olive oil and season with salt and black pepper. 3. Place the salmon fillets skin-side down on the grill.
4. Cook for 6 to 8 minutes on each side or until the salmon is opaque and flakes easily with a fork.
5. Remove from the grill and serve immediately with lemon wedges on the side.

SERVES
4

PREP TIME
10

METHOD
Grilling

COOK TIME
15

INGREDIENTS

- 4 salmon fillets (6 ounces each)
- 2 tablespoons olive oil
- 1 tablespoon fresh lemon juice
- 1 teaspoon lemon zest

- 2 tablespoons fresh dill, chopped.
- Salt and freshly ground black pepper to taste.
- Lemon wedges for serving.

NUTRITIONAL INFORMATION

320 calories, 34 g protein, 1 g carbohydrates, 20 g fat, 0 g fiber, 85 mg cholesterol, 85 mg sodium, 600 mg potassium.

SHRIMP SAGANAKI

SERVES
4

PREP TIME
15

METHOD
Simmering

COOK TIME
20

DIRECTIONS

1. Warm the olive oil in a large skillet over medium heat. Add the chopped onion and simmer for about 5 minutes or until softened. Cook the garlic for a further minute after adding it.

2. Add the red pepper flakes, dry oregano, white wine, and diced tomatoes with their juices—season with pepper and salt. After bringing it to a simmer, the sauce begins its gradual thickening process, a satisfying transformation that takes about ten minutes.

3. Add the shrimp to the skillet and toss to coat them evenly with sauce. Simmer the shrimp for 4–5 minutes or until they are opaque and pink.

4. Turn off the heat and scatter the feta cheese crumbles on the skillet. To soften the cheese, cover the skillet and let it sit for two minutes.

5. Before serving, garnish with freshly cut parsley.

INGREDIENTS

- 1-pound large shrimp, peeled and deveined
- 2 tablespoons olive oil
- 1 small onion finely chopped.
- 3 cloves garlic, minced.
- 1 can (14.5 ounces) diced tomatoes.
- 1/4 cup dry white wine
- 1/2 teaspoon dried oregano
- 1/2 teaspoon red pepper flakes
- Salt and freshly ground black pepper to taste.
- 4 ounces feta cheese, crumbled.
- 2 tablespoons chopped fresh parsley

NUTRITIONAL INFORMATION

280 calories, 24 g protein, 10 g carbohydrates, 15 g fat, 2 g fiber, 160 mg cholesterol, 710 mg sodium, 420 mg potassium.

MEDITERRANEAN BAKED COD

SERVES
4

PREP TIME
10

METHOD
Baking

COOK TIME
25

DIRECTIONS

1. Preheat the oven to 400°F or 200°C. Mix the lemon juice, olive oil, thyme, oregano, and minced garlic in a small bowl.

2. Now, let's bring in the freshness. Transfer the cod fillets, red onion slices, cherry tomatoes, and Kalamata olives to an ovenproof tray. The vibrant colors and flavors are about to come alive!

3. Drizzle the cod and veggies with the olive oil mixture. To taste, add salt and pepper for seasoning.

4. Bake for 20 to 25 minutes until the fish flakes easily with a fork and is opaque. Before serving, garnish with fresh parsley.

INGREDIENTS

- 4 cod fillets (6 ounces each)
- 1/4 cup extra virgin olive oil
- 2 tablespoons lemon juice
- 1 teaspoon dried oregano
- 1 teaspoon dried thyme
- 3 garlic cloves, minced.
- 1-pint cherry tomatoes, halved
- 1/4 cup Kalamata olives pitted and halved.
- 1 small red onion thinly sliced.
- Salt and freshly ground black pepper to taste.
- 1/4 cup fresh parsley, chopped (for garnish)

NUTRITIONAL INFORMATION

280 calories, 30 g protein, 8 g carbohydrates, 14 g fat, 2 g fiber, 75 mg cholesterol, 400 mg sodium, 700 mg potassium.

SEAFOOD PAELLA

DIRECTIONS

1. Heat the olive oil over medium heat in a large skillet or paella pan. Saute the chopped onion and bell pepper for approximately five minutes or until tender. Add the minced garlic and cook for an extra minute.

2. Once the veggies are ready, toss to coat the rice in the oil and veggies. Then, stir in the Arborio rice, saffron strands, and smoked paprika. The addition of the seafood stock is crucial as it brings out the flavors of the dish. Heat until it boils. Simmer, uncovered, over medium-low heat for fifteen minutes without stirring.

3. Arrange the calamari, shrimp, and mussels on top of the rice, pressing them a little bit into the liquid. Simmer for 10 to 15 minutes or until the rice is soft and the fish is thoroughly cooked. In the final five minutes of cooking, add the frozen peas.

4. Once the cooking is complete, remove the pan from the burner and cover it with a fresh dishtowel. This step is important as it allows the paella to rest for five minutes, giving the flavors a chance to meld and the dish to set. Before serving, add lemon wedges and finely chopped fresh parsley as garnish. To taste, add salt and pepper for seasoning.

SERVES
4

PREP TIME
15

METHOD
Sautéing-
Simmering

30
25

INGREDIENTS

- 2 tablespoons extra virgin olive oil
- 1 small onion finely chopped.
- 1 bell pepper (red or green), chopped.
- 2 cloves garlic, minced.
- 1 cup Arborio rice
- 1/4 teaspoon saffron threads
- 1/2 teaspoon smoked paprika.

- 4 cups seafood stock
- 8 ounces large shrimp peeled and deveined.
- 8 ounces mussels scrubbed and debearded.
- 8 ounces calamari rings
- 1 cup frozen peas
- 1/4 cup chopped fresh parsley.
- 1 lemon, cut into wedges.

NUTRITIONAL INFORMATION

380 calories, 26 g protein, 42 g carbohydrates, 12 g fat, 3 g fiber, 115 mg cholesterol, 790 mg sodium, 450 mg potassium.

BAKED RED SNAPPER

SERVES
4

PREP TIME
10

METHOD
Baking

COOK TIME
25

DIRECTIONS

1. Preheat the oven to 400°F or 200°C. Grease a baking dish with a small amount of olive oil.

2. Place the red snapper fillets in the baking dish. Drizzle with olive oil and sprinkle with minced garlic.

3. Enhance the flavor of each fillet by adding fresh lemon slices, aromatic dried oregano, and vibrant chopped parsley. Season with a pinch of salt and pepper. For a burst of color, arrange sliced red onion and juicy cherry tomatoes around the fish.

4. Bake in a preheated oven for 20 to 25 minutes, or until a fork can easily pierce the fish.

5. Garnish the cooked red snapper, if preferred, with extra fresh parsley.

INGREDIENTS

- 4 red snapper fillets (about 6 ounces each)
- 1/4 cup extra virgin olive oil
- 2 cloves garlic, minced.
- 1 lemon thinly sliced.
- 1/4 cup fresh parsley, chopped.

- 1 teaspoon dried oregano
- Salt and freshly ground black pepper to taste.
- 1/2 cup cherry tomatoes, halved.
- 1 small red onion thinly sliced.

NUTRITIONAL INFORMATION

310 calories, 35 g protein, 8 g carbohydrates, 16 g fat, 2 g fiber, 70 mg cholesterol, 320 mg sodium, 750 mg potassium.

BAKED COD WITH TOMATOES AND OLIVES

SERVES
4

PREP TIME
10

METHOD
Baking

COOK TIME
25

DIRECTIONS

1. Preheat the oven to 400°F or 200°C. Grease a baking dish with a small amount of olive oil.

2. Place the cod fillets in the baking dish. Add sliced red onion, Kalamata olives, and cherry tomatoes to the area surrounding the fish. Sprinkle some minced garlic on top.

3. Drizzle the fish and veggies with olive oil. Season with black pepper, salt, and dried oregano.

4. Bake the fish for 20 to 25 minutes in a preheated oven or until it is opaque and flakes readily with a fork.

5. To finish off, add a dollop of fresh parsley on top of the beautifully baked fish and serve it with wedges of lemon. The vibrant colors and fresh flavors are sure to inspire your taste buds!

INGREDIENTS

- 1 1/2 pounds cod fillets
- 2 cups cherry tomatoes, halved.
- 1/2 cup Kalamata olives pitted and halved.
- 1 small red onion thinly sliced.
- 3 cloves garlic, minced.
- 2 tablespoons extra virgin olive oil
- 1 teaspoon dried oregano
- 1/2 teaspoon salt
- 1/4 teaspoon black pepper
- 1/4 cup fresh parsley, chopped.
- 1 lemon, cut into wedges.

NUTRITIONAL INFORMATION

270 calories, 30 g protein, 10 g carbohydrates, 12 g fat, 3 g fiber, 70 mg cholesterol, 600 mg sodium, 750 mg potassium.

SALMON AND ASPARAGUS

SERVES
4

PREP TIME
10

METHOD
Baking

COOK TIME
15

DIRECTIONS

1. Set the oven's temperature to 400°F or 200°C. Use parchment paper to line a baking sheet.
2. Place the asparagus and salmon fillets on the prepared baking sheet. Add lemon juice and olive oil.
3. Season the salmon and asparagus with salt, pepper, dried oregano, and minced garlic.
4. In a preheated oven, Bake for 12 to 15 minutes or until the asparagus is soft and the salmon is cooked. Accompany with wedges of lemon.

INGREDIENTS

- 4 salmon fillets (6 ounces each)
- 1 bunch asparagus, trimmed.
- 3 tablespoons olive oil
- 2 tablespoons lemon juice
- 2 cloves garlic, minced.
- 1 teaspoon dried oregano
- Salt and freshly ground black pepper to taste.
- Lemon wedges, for serving.

NUTRITIONAL INFORMATION

350 calories, 34 g protein, 7 g carbohydrates, 21 g fat, 3 g fiber, 75 mg cholesterol, 100 mg sodium, 750 mg potassium.

BAKED TILAPIA WITH LEMON

SERVES
4

PREP TIME
10

METHOD
Baking

COOK TIME
20

DIRECTIONS

1. Preheat your oven to 375°F (190°C). Lightly grease a baking dish with one tablespoon of olive oil.

2. Arrange the tilapia fillets in the prepared baking dish. Drizzle the remaining olive oil over the fillets.

3. Sprinkle dried oregano, dried thyme, garlic powder, salt, and pepper evenly over the fish. Top each fillet with lemon slices.

4. After baking in the oven for 20 minutes or until the fish flakes easily with a fork, your dish is almost complete. But wait, there's one more step to add that final touch. Garnish with fresh parsley before serving. Now, it's ready to be enjoyed!

INGREDIENTS

- 4 tilapia fillets (about 4 ounces each)
- 2 tablespoons olive oil
- 1 lemon, thinly sliced
- 1 teaspoon dried oregano
- 1 teaspoon dried thyme
- 1/2 teaspoon garlic powder
- Salt and freshly ground black pepper to taste
- 2 tablespoons fresh parsley, chopped.

NUTRITIONAL INFORMATION

210 calories, 28 g protein, 2 g carbohydrates, 10 g fat, 1 g fiber, 70 mg cholesterol, 230 mg sodium, 400 mg potassium.

FISH AND VEGETABLE SKEWERS

DIRECTIONS

1. Combine the olive oil, lemon juice, minced garlic, dried oregano, salt, and pepper in a big bowl. Toss to coat after adding the fish cubes and veggies. Let it marinate for fifteen minutes.
2. Set the grill's temperature to medium-high. Alternately, thread the veggies and fish onto the skewers.
3. Turn the skewers once or twice while grilling them for ten to fifteen minutes or until the fish is cooked and the vegetables are soft.
4. Serve right away.

SERVES
4

PREP TIME
20

METHOD
Grilling

COOK TIME
15

INGREDIENTS

- 1 pound firm white fish (such as cod or halibut), cut into 1-inch cubes
- 1 red bell pepper, cut into 1-inch pieces
- 1 yellow bell pepper, cut into 1-inch pieces
- 1 zucchini, sliced into 1/2-inch rounds
- 1 red onion, cut into wedges
- 1/4 cup extra virgin olive oil
- 2 tablespoons lemon juice
- 2 cloves garlic, minced
- 1 teaspoon dried oregano
- Salt and freshly ground black pepper to taste
- 8 wooden skewers, soaked in water for 30 minutes

NUTRITIONAL INFORMATION

280 calories, 24 g protein, 10 g carbohydrates, 16 g fat, 3 g fiber, 45 mg cholesterol, 160 mg sodium, 600 mg potassium.

LEMON GARLIC MUSSELS

SERVES
4

PREP TIME
10

METHOD
Simmering

COOK TIME
10

DIRECTIONS

1. Heat the olive oil in a big pot over medium heat. Add the minced garlic and cook for one minute or until fragrant.

2. Fill the saucepan with the white wine, lemon juice, and, if desired, red pepper flakes. Heat through to a simmer.

3. After adding the mussels to the pot, simmer them for five to seven minutes or until they have opened. Discard any that do not open.

4. Add the chopped parsley, taste, and adjust the seasoning with salt and black pepper. Serve right away.

INGREDIENTS

- 2 pounds fresh mussels, cleaned and debearded
- 2 tablespoons olive oil
- 4 garlic cloves, minced
- 1/2 cup dry white wine
- 1 lemon, juiced
- 1/4 teaspoon red pepper flakes (optional)
- 1/4 cup fresh parsley, chopped
- Salt and freshly ground black pepper to taste

NUTRITIONAL INFORMATION

220 calories, 22 g protein, 8 g carbohydrates, 10 g fat, 0 g fiber, 45 mg cholesterol, 520 mg sodium, 550 mg potassium.

GRILLED SWORDFISH STEAKS

SERVES
4

PREP TIME
10

METHOD
Grilling

COOK TIME
15

DIRECTIONS

1. In a small bowl, combine the olive oil, lemon juice, dried oregano, minced garlic, salt, and pepper.

2. Transfer the swordfish steaks to a shallow plate and cover them with marinade. Let the steaks marinate for ten minutes.

3. Set the grill's temperature to medium-high. The swordfish steaks should be cooked on the grill for 4–5 minutes on each side or until the flesh is opaque and flakes readily. Patience is key here, as it ensures a perfectly cooked steak.

4. Remove the meat from the grill and let it rest for a few minutes. Garnish with chopped fresh parsley and serve with lemon wedges. .

INGREDIENTS

- 4 swordfish steaks (about 6 ounces each)
- 1/4 cup extra virgin olive oil
- 2 tablespoons lemon juice
- 2 cloves garlic, minced.
- 1 teaspoon dried oregano
- Salt and freshly ground black pepper to taste.
- Lemon wedges for serving.
- Fresh parsley, chopped, for garnish.

NUTRITIONAL INFORMATION

320 calories, 35 g protein, 1 g carbohydrates, 20 g fat, 0 g fiber, 70 mg cholesterol, 200 mg sodium, 700 mg potassium.

PAN-SEARED SCALLOPS

SERVES
4

PREP TIME
10

METHOD
Sautéing

COOK TIME
10

DIRECTIONS

1. Pat the scallops dry with paper towels, then season them on both sides with salt and black pepper.

2. Heat the olive oil in a large skillet over medium-high heat. Add the minced garlic and simmer for one minute or until fragrant.

3. Here's a pro tip: when adding the scallops to the skillet, make sure to pack them in a manageable amount. This will ensure even cooking. Cook for 2 to 3 minutes on each side until they turn a delicious golden brown.

4. Take the scallops out of the skillet and give them a quick squeeze of lemon juice. Before serving, sprinkle with chopped parsley. Accompany with wedges of lemon.

INGREDIENTS

- 1 pound sea scallops
- 2 tablespoons extra virgin olive oil
- 1 clove garlic, minced
- 1/4 cup fresh lemon juice
- 1/4 cup chopped fresh parsley
- Salt and freshly ground black pepper to taste
- Lemon wedges for serving

NUTRITIONAL INFORMATION

180 calories, 20 g protein, 4 g carbohydrates, 9 g fat, 1 g fiber, 35 mg cholesterol, 320 mg sodium, 450 mg potassium.

CHAPTER 07
Main Dishes

GREEK CHICKEN SOUVLAKI

SERVES
4

PREP TIME
10

METHOD
Grilling

COOK TIME
20

DIRECTIONS

1. In a big bowl, combine the olive oil, lemon juice, minced garlic, dried thyme, dried oregano, salt, and pepper. Add the cubed chicken and toss to coat. Cover and chill for at least fifteen minutes to marinate.

2. Turn the heat to medium-high on a grill or grill pan. Thread the marinated chicken, red onion, and bell pepper pieces onto the soaked skewers, alternating between chicken and vegetables.

3. Cook the skewers for 8 to 10 minutes, rotating them now and then until the chicken is nicely grilled and cooked through.

4. Take off the grill and serve immediately with your preferred sides.

INGREDIENTS

- 1 1/2 pounds boneless, skinless chicken breast, cut into 1-inch cubes
- 3 tablespoons olive oil
- 2 tablespoons lemon juice
- 2 cloves garlic, minced
- 1 teaspoon dried oregano
- 1/2 teaspoon dried thyme
- 1/2 teaspoon salt
- 1/4 teaspoon freshly ground black pepper
- 1 red onion, cut into 1-inch pieces
- 1 bell pepper (any color), cut into 1-inch pieces
- 8 wooden skewers (soaked in water for 30 minutes)

NUTRITIONAL INFORMATION

280 calories, 32 g protein, 6 g carbohydrates, 14 g fat, 2 g fiber, 75 mg cholesterol, 350 mg sodium, 450 mg potassium.

GARLIC AND HERB GRILLED LAMB CHOPS

DIRECTIONS

1. In a small bowl, combine the minced garlic, olive oil, salt, pepper, thyme, and rosemary to make the marinade.

2. Apply the marinade to the lamb chops, coating them well. Let them marinate for at least fifteen minutes.

3. Set the grill's temperature to medium-high. To achieve medium-rare, grill the lamb chops on each side for [4–5 minutes per side] or until done to your preference.

4. Remove the lamb chops from the grill and let them rest. Drizzle lemon juice over them before serving.

SERVES
4

PREP TIME
10

METHOD
Grilling

COOK TIME
15

INGREDIENTS

- 8 lamb chops (about 1 inch thick)
- 3 cloves garlic, minced
- 1/4 cup fresh rosemary, finely chopped
- 1/4 cup fresh thyme, finely chopped
- 1/4 cup fresh parsley, finely chopped
- 1/4 cup extra virgin olive oil
- 1 teaspoon salt
- 1/2 teaspoon freshly ground black pepper
- Juice of 1 lemon

NUTRITIONAL INFORMATION

420 calories, 30 g protein, 2 g carbohydrates, 32 g fat, 0 g fiber, 95 mg cholesterol, 380 mg sodium, 430 mg potassium.

ITALIAN SHRIMP PASTA

SERVES
4

PREP TIME
15

METHOD
Sautéing-
Simmering

COOK TIME
20

DIRECTIONS

1. Cook the pasta until al dente, following the directions on the package. After draining, set away.

2. Heat the olive oil in a big skillet over medium-high heat. Add the red pepper flakes and garlic, and cook for one minute or until fragrant.

3. When the shrimp are pink and opaque, add them to the skillet and cook them for two to three minutes on each side. Take out and place aside the shrimp from the skillet.

4. Add the cherry tomatoes to the same skillet and simmer for 5 minutes or until they soften. After adding the white wine, simmer for two to three minutes.

5. Add the cooked spaghetti back to the skillet with the shrimp and toss to mix. Add the grated Parmesan cheese and chopped basil, and stir. To taste, add salt and pepper for seasoning. Serve right away.

INGREDIENTS

- 8 ounces whole wheat spaghetti
- 1 pound large shrimp, peeled and deveined
- 2 tablespoons extra virgin olive oil
- 4 cloves garlic, minced
- 1/2 teaspoon red pepper flakes
- 1 pint cherry tomatoes, halved
- 1/2 cup dry white wine
- 1/4 cup chopped fresh basil
- 1/4 cup grated Parmesan cheese
- Salt and freshly ground black pepper to taste

NUTRITIONAL INFORMATION

400 calories, 28 g protein, 45 g carbohydrates, 12 g fat, 6 g fiber, 175 mg cholesterol, 580 mg sodium, 420 mg potassium.

ITALIAN CAPRESE STUFFED PEPPERS

DIRECTIONS

1. Preheat the oven to 375°F. Slice off the bell peppers' tops, removing the seeds and membranes. Place the peppers on a baking tray.
2. Combine the chopped basil, mozzarella cubes, and cherry tomatoes in a large bowl. Drizzle with olive oil and season with pepper and salt. Toss to mix.
3. Stuff the tomato and mozzarella mixture into each bell pepper.
4. Bake in a preheated oven for 20 minutes or until the cheese is melted and the peppers are soft.
5. Before serving, drizzle with balsamic glaze.

SERVES
4

PREP TIME
15

METHOD
Grilling

COOK TIME
20

INGREDIENTS

- 4 large bell peppers (any color)
- 2 cups cherry tomatoes, halved
- 8 ounces fresh mozzarella, cubed
- 1/2 cup fresh basil leaves, chopped
- 3 tablespoons balsamic glaze
- 2 tablespoons extra virgin olive oil
- Salt and freshly ground black pepper to taste

NUTRITIONAL INFORMATION

220 calories, 10 g protein, 14 g carbohydrates, 14 g fat, 3 g fiber, 40 mg cholesterol, 250 mg sodium, 350 mg potassium.

ITALIAN MOROCCAN RED LENTIL AND PUMPKIN STEW

DIRECTIONS

1. Sauté the Aromatics: Heat the olive oil in a big pot over medium heat. Sauté the onion and garlic for around five minutes or until tender.

2. Add Pumpkin and Spices: Mix turmeric, cinnamon, smoked paprika, cumin, and coriander. Simmer for one minute or until aromatic. Cook, stirring occasionally, for an additional five minutes after adding the diced pumpkin.

3. Mix the Ingredients: Add the chickpeas, diced tomatoes, vegetable broth, and red lentils. After bringing it to a boil, lower the heat, and simmer the lentils and pumpkin for 30 to 35 minutes or until soft.

4. Season and Serve: Add pepper and salt to taste. If desired, garnish with finely chopped cilantro. Serve hot.

SERVES
4

PREP TIME
15

METHOD
Simmering

COOK TIME
45

INGREDIENTS

- ·2 tablespoons olive oil
- ·1 medium onion, diced
- ·2 cloves garlic, minced
- ·1 teaspoon ground cumin
- ·1 teaspoon ground coriander
- ·1 teaspoon smoked paprika
- ·1/2 teaspoon ground cinnamon
- ·1/2 teaspoon ground turmeric
- ·1 cup red lentils, rinsed

- ·2 cups diced pumpkin (about 1 pound)
- ·4 cups vegetable broth
- ·1 can (14.5 ounces) diced tomatoes
- ·1 can (15 ounces) chickpeas, drained and rinsed
- ·1/4 cup chopped fresh cilantro (optional, for garnish)
- ·Salt and pepper to taste

NUTRITIONAL INFORMATION

320 calories, 14g protein, 48g carbohydrates, 8g fat, 12g fiber, 0mg cholesterol, 640mg sodium, 950mg potassium.

80

FARRO WITH ROASTED TOMATOES AND MUSHROOMS

DIRECTIONS

1. Prepare the Farro: Rinse it well with cold water. Combine the water and farro in a medium saucepan. Bring to a boil, then lower the heat and simmer until soft, about 30 minutes. Remove any extra water.

2. To Roast Vegetables, Set the Oven Temperature to 400°F. On a baking sheet, combine cherry tomatoes and mushrooms with garlic, olive oil, thyme, oregano, salt, and pepper. Roast until soft and beginning to caramelize about 20 minutes.

3. Finally, it's time to enjoy our creation. Mix the cooked farro, roasted tomatoes, and mushrooms in a big bowl. Add the fresh basil and Parmesan cheese and stir. If necessary, add more salt and pepper to the seasoning. Serve hot and savor the delicious flavors of the farro and roasted vegetables.

SERVES
4

PREP TIME
10

METHOD
Simmering-
Roasting

COOK TIME
50

INGREDIENTS

- 1 cup farro
- 2 cups water
- 1 pint cherry tomatoes, halved
- 8 oz mushrooms, sliced
- 2 tbsp extra virgin olive oil
- 1 tsp salt
- 1/2 tsp black pepper
- 1/2 tsp dried thyme
- 1/2 tsp dried oregano
- 2 cloves garlic, minced
- 1/4 cup grated Parmesan cheese
- 2 tbsp chopped fresh basil

NUTRITIONAL INFORMATION

320 calories, 10g protein, 45g carbohydrates, 12g fat, 7g fiber, 5mg cholesterol, 500mg sodium, 500mg potassium.

STUFFED PORTOBELLOS

SERVES
4

PREP TIME
15

METHOD
Baking

COOK TIME
25

DIRECTIONS

1. Preheat the oven to 375°F or 190°C. Slice the stems off the portobello mushrooms and drizzle some olive oil over the caps. With the gills facing up, put them on a baking sheet.

2. Sauté the onion and garlic in the remaining olive oil in a skillet over medium heat for about five minutes or until the onion is transparent. Cook the sun-dried tomatoes and chopped spinach for two to three minutes or until the spinach has wilted.

3. Turn off the heat and mix in the breadcrumbs and feta cheese. To taste, add salt and pepper for seasoning. Evenly distribute the mixture among the mushroom tops.

4. Bake for 20 minutes, or until the mushrooms are soft and the tops are browned, in a preheated oven. Serve hot.

INGREDIENTS

- 4 large Portobello mushrooms
- 2 tablespoons olive oil
- 1 small onion, finely chopped
- 2 cloves garlic, minced
- 1 cup fresh spinach, chopped
- 1/2 cup sun-dried tomatoes, chopped
- 1/2 cup crumbled feta cheese
- 1/4 cup breadcrumbs
- Salt and pepper to taste

NUTRITIONAL INFORMATION

180 calories, 6g protein, 14g carbohydrates, 12g fat, 3g fiber, 15mg cholesterol, 350mg sodium, 400mg potassium.

CREAMY CHICKPEA SAUCE WITH WHOLE-WHEAT FUSILLI

DIRECTIONS

1. Prepare the fusilli pasta per the directions on the package. After draining, set away.

2. Put the chickpeas, lemon juice, Parmesan cheese, olive oil, and vegetable broth in a blender. Blend till creamy and smooth.

3. Add the creamy chickpea sauce and cooked pasta to a large pan set over medium heat. Cook, stirring periodically, for 5 to 7 minutes or until thoroughly cooked. To taste, add salt and pepper for seasoning.

4. Before serving, garnish with fresh parsley.

SERVES
4

PREP TIME
10

METHOD
Boiling-
Blending

COOK TIME
20

INGREDIENTS

- 12 oz whole-wheat fusilli pasta
- 1 can (15 oz) chickpeas, drained and rinsed
- 1/4 cup extra-virgin olive oil
- 1/2 cup vegetable broth
- 3 cloves garlic, minced
- 1/4 cup grated Parmesan cheese
- 1/4 cup fresh parsley, chopped
- 1 lemon, juiced
- Salt and pepper to taste

NUTRITIONAL INFORMATION

450 calories, 14g protein, 67g carbohydrates, 14g fat, 12g fiber, 10mg cholesterol, 300mg sodium, 470mg potassium.

ROASTED VEGETABLE AND HUMMUS WRAP

SERVES
4

PREP TIME
15

METHOD
Roasting

COOK TIME
25

DIRECTIONS

1. Preheat Oven: Set the oven's temperature to 400°F.
2. Roast Vegetables: Combine olive oil, oregano, salt, and pepper with bell peppers, zucchini, and red onion on a baking sheet. Arrange the veggies in a single layer and roast for twenty to twenty-five minutes or until they are soft and have a hint of caramel.
3. Assemble Wraps: Top each tortilla with 1/4 cup of hummus. Garnish with feta cheese, roasted veggies, and a few spinach leaves, if desired. To make wraps, neatly roll the tortillas.
4. Serve: Halve every wrapper and present it right away.

INGREDIENTS

- 2 cups mixed bell peppers, sliced
- 1 medium zucchini, sliced
- 1 medium red onion, sliced
- 2 tablespoons olive oil
- 1 teaspoon dried oregano
- 1/2 teaspoon salt

- 1/4 teaspoon black pepper
- 1 cup hummus
- 4 whole wheat tortillas
- 1 cup fresh spinach leaves
- 1/2 cup crumbled feta cheese (optional)

NUTRITIONAL INFORMATION

280 calories, 8g protein, 36g carbohydrates, 12g fat, 8g fiber, omg cholesterol, 500mg sodium, 520mg potassium.

84

MEDITERRANEAN BAKED CHICKEN THIGHS

SERVES
4

PREP TIME
10

METHOD
Roasting

COOK TIME
35

DIRECTIONS

1. Set oven temperature to 400°F. Put the chicken thighs in an ovenproof dish.
In a small bowl, create a flavorful blend of olive oil, garlic, thyme, oregano, salt, and pepper. Gently massage this aromatic mixture onto the chicken thighs, ensuring every inch is coated.
2. Sprinkle the Kalamata olives and lemon slices all over the chicken. Bake the chicken for thirty to thirty-five minutes or until it is cooked through and golden brown.
3. Before serving, garnish with fresh parsley.

INGREDIENTS

- 8 bone-in, skin-on chicken thighs
- 2 tablespoons extra virgin olive oil
- 1 lemon, thinly sliced
- 1/4 cup Kalamata olives, pitted
- 3 cloves garlic, minced

- 1 teaspoon dried oregano
- 1 teaspoon dried thyme
- Salt and freshly ground black pepper to taste
- 1/4 cup fresh parsley, chopped

NUTRITIONAL INFORMATION

350 calories, 28 g protein, 4 g carbohydrates, 24 g fat, 1 g fiber, 110 mg cholesterol, 520 mg sodium, 400 mg potassium.

MEDITERRANEAN STUFFED ZUCCHINI BOATS

SERVES
4

PREP TIME
20

METHOD
Sautéing-
Baking

COOK TIME
30

DIRECTIONS

1. Set oven temperature to 375°F. Transfer the halves of zucchini to a baking dish.
 Heat the olive oil in a big skillet over medium heat. Add the onion and garlic, and simmer for three minutes or until softened.

2. Add the ground turkey and, using a spoon to break it up, heat until browned. Add the oregano, olives, cherry tomatoes, salt, and pepper and stir. Simmer for five more minutes.

3. Divide the turkey mixture among the two pieces of zucchini. Add some crumbled feta cheese on top.

4. Bake the zucchini for 25 to 30 minutes or until soft. Garnish with fresh basil before serving.

INGREDIENTS

- 4 medium zucchinis, halved lengthwise and seeds scooped out
- 1/2 pound ground turkey
- 1 small red onion, finely chopped
- 2 cloves garlic, minced
- 1 cup cherry tomatoes, halved
- 1/4 cup Kalamata olives, chopped
- 1/4 cup crumbled feta cheese
- 1 teaspoon dried oregano
- 1 tablespoon extra-virgin olive oil
- Salt and freshly ground black pepper to taste
- 1/4 cup fresh basil, chopped

NUTRITIONAL INFORMATION

180 calories, 20 g protein, 4 g carbohydrates, 9 g fat, 1 g fiber, 35 mg cholesterol, 320 mg sodium, 450 mg potassium.

MEDITERRANEAN RATATOUILLE

DIRECTIONS

1. Preheat the oven to 375°F. Add the bell peppers, onion, garlic, zucchini, eggplant, and yellow squash to a large baking dish.
2. Add olive oil and season with salt, pepper, oregano, and thyme. Toss to coat the vegetables evenly.
3. Add the chopped tomatoes to the veggies and toss to mix. Bake the dish for thirty minutes with the foil covering it. Remove the foil after 15 more minutes of baking or until the vegetables are soft.
4. Before serving, garnish with fresh basil.

SERVES
4

PREP TIME
15

METHOD
Roasting

COOK TIME
45

INGREDIENTS

- 1 large eggplant, diced
- 1 zucchini, sliced
- 1 yellow squash, sliced
- 1 red bell pepper, chopped
- 1 yellow bell pepper, chopped
- 1 large onion, chopped
- 4 cloves garlic, minced
- 1 can (14.5 ounces) diced tomatoes
- 2 tablespoons extra virgin olive oil
- 1 teaspoon dried thyme
- 1 teaspoon dried oregano
- Salt and freshly ground black pepper to taste
- 1/4 cup fresh basil, chopped

NUTRITIONAL INFORMATION

180 calories, 4 g protein, 28 g carbohydrates, 7 g fat, 8 g fiber, 0 mg cholesterol, 400 mg sodium, 750 mg potassium.

CHAPTER 08
Desserts

POACHED PEARS IN RED WINE

SERVES
4

PREP TIME
15

METHOD
Roasting

COOK TIME
30

DIRECTIONS

1. Combine the red wine, water, split vanilla bean, cloves, cinnamon sticks, and granulated sugar in a big pot. Over medium heat, bring the mixture to a simmer and stir until the sugar dissolves.

2. Fill the pot with the peeled and cored pears. Verify that they are entirely immersed in the liquid. Add extra wine or water as needed.

3. Lower the temperature to a simmer and poach the pears for twenty to thirty minutes or until a fork pierces them easily. To guarantee equal cooking, turn the pears from time to time.

4. Remove the pears from the saucepan and simmer the poaching liquid for ten more minutes or until it reduces significantly. Drizzle the pears with the decreased poaching liquid and serve warm or cold.

INGREDIENTS

- 4 firm pears, peeled and cored
- 2 cups red wine (such as Merlot or Cabernet Sauvignon)
- 1 cup water

- 1 cup granulated sugar
- 1 cinnamon stick
- 2 cloves
- 1 orange, zested
- 1 vanilla bean, split

NUTRITIONAL INFORMATION

210 calories, 1g protein, 50g carbohydrates, 0g fat, 5g fiber, 0mg cholesterol, 5mg sodium, 220mg potassium.

BAKED APPLES WITH CINNAMON AND HONEY

DIRECTIONS

1. Preheat the oven to 175°C or 350°F. Core the apples, leaving a half-inch margin at the bottom to accommodate the filling.
2. Combine the nutmeg, cinnamon, and honey in a small bowl. If using, add the chopped raisins and walnuts to the mixture.
3. Press the honey mixture firmly into the center of each apple. Pour the water into the bottom of the baking dish with the apples inside.
4. Bake in an oven for 30 minutes or until the filling is bubbling and the apples are soft. The final step is to serve this warm, delicious dish to your loved ones, basking in a sense of accomplishment. .

SERVES
4

PREP TIME
15

METHOD
Baking

COOK TIME
30

INGREDIENTS

- 4 medium apples (e.g., Honeycrisp or Gala)
- 1/4 cup honey
- 1 teaspoon ground cinnamon
- 1/4 teaspoon ground nutmeg
- 1/4 cup chopped walnuts (optional)
- 1/4 cup raisins (optional)
- 1/2 cup water

NUTRITIONAL INFORMATION

220 calories, 1g protein, 57g carbohydrates, 1g fat, 5g fiber, 0mg cholesterol, 5mg sodium, 200mg potassium.

GRILLED PEACHES WITH GREEK YOGURT

DIRECTIONS

1. Turn the heat up to medium-high on the grill.
2. Apply some olive oil to the peach halves.
3. Arrange the peaches on the grill, cut side down. Grill the peaches for 4–5 minutes or until they have grill marks and are starting to soften.
4. Take the peaches off the barbecue. Top each half of a peach with a dollop of Greek yogurt, a honey drizzle, and a dusting of ground cinnamon. If desired, garnish with fresh mint leaves.

SERVES
4

PREP TIME
10

METHOD
Grilling

COOK TIME
10

INGREDIENTS

- 4 ripe peaches, halved and pitted
- 1 tablespoon olive oil
- 2 cups plain Greek yogurt

- 2 tablespoons honey
- 1 teaspoon ground cinnamon
- Fresh mint leaves for garnish (optional)

NUTRITIONAL INFORMATION

150 calories, 6g protein, 20g carbohydrates, 5g fat, 2g fiber, 0mg cholesterol, 30mg sodium, 290mg potassium.

BERRY AND MINT SALAD

DIRECTIONS

1. Put raspberries, blueberries, and strawberries in a big basin.
2. Gently toss the berries and mint in the basin after adding the chopped leaves.
3. Mix the lemon juice and honey in a small bowl until thoroughly blended.
4. Lightly toss to ensure uniform coating after drizzling the honey-lemon mixture over the fruit and mint salad.

SERVES
4

PREP TIME
10

METHOD
NO-COOK

COOK TIME
0

INGREDIENTS

- 1 cup strawberries, hulled and sliced
- 1 cup blueberries
- 1 cup raspberries

- 1/4 cup fresh mint leaves, chopped
- 2 tablespoons honey
- 1 tablespoon lemon juice

NUTRITIONAL INFORMATION

110 calories, 1g protein, 28g carbohydrates, 0.5g fat, 7g fiber, 0mg cholesterol, 5mg sodium, 260mg potassium.

BAKED FIGS WITH HONEY AND ALMONDS

DIRECTIONS

1. Turn the oven on to 375°F, or 190°C. Use parchment paper to line a baking sheet.

2. Cut the figs in half lengthwise after rinsing them. Arrange the figs on the prepared baking sheet and cut side up.

3. Evenly drizzle the figs with honey, then top with ground cinnamon and chopped almonds. Lastly, drizzle the figs with the melted butter.

4. Bake for 15 minutes, or until the almonds are golden brown and the figs are soft, in a preheated oven. Serve warm.

SERVES
4

PREP TIME
10

METHOD
Baking

COOK TIME
15

INGREDIENTS

- 8 fresh figs
- 2 tablespoons honey
- 1/4 cup sliced almonds

- 1 teaspoon ground cinnamon
- 1 tablespoon unsalted butter, melted

NUTRITIONAL INFORMATION

150 calories, 2g protein, 25g carbohydrates, 6g fat, 4g fiber, 0mg cholesterol, 5mg sodium, 150mg potassium.

OLIVE OIL AND ALMOND CAKE

DIRECTIONS

1. Set the oven's temperature to 350°F. Use olive oil to grease a 9-inch round cake pan.

2. Combine the whole wheat flour, almond flour, baking soda, baking powder, and salt in a medium-sized basin.

3. Beat the eggs, applesauce, honey, almond extract, vanilla extract, and olive oil in a big basin until thoroughly mixed.

4. Mixing until just incorporated, gradually add the dry ingredients to the wet components. Transfer the mixture to the ready-made cake pan.

5. Bake for 35 minutes or until the middle comes out clear when a toothpick is inserted. After letting the cake set in the pan for ten minutes, move it to a wire rack to finish cooling.

SERVES
4

PREP TIME
15

METHOD
Baking

COOK TIME
35

INGREDIENTS

- 1 cup almond flour
- 1/2 cup whole wheat flour
- 1/2 teaspoon baking powder
- 1/4 teaspoon baking soda
- 1/4 teaspoon salt
- 1/2 cup extra-virgin olive oil
- 1/2 cup unsweetened applesauce
- 3 large eggs
- 1 teaspoon vanilla extract
- 1/2 teaspoon almond extract
- 1/4 cup honey

NUTRITIONAL INFORMATION

350 calories, 28 g protein, 4 g carbohydrates, 24 g fat, 1 g fiber, 110 mg cholesterol, 520 mg sodium, 400 mg potassium.

RICOTTA AND HONEY TARTLETS

SERVES
4

PREP TIME
15

METHOD
Baking

COOK TIME
20

DIRECTIONS

1. Preheat oven to 375°F (190°C). Roll out the puff pastry sheet on a lightly floured surface and cut it into four equal squares. Place the squares on a baking sheet lined with parchment paper.
2. Mix the ricotta cheese, honey, vanilla extract, and lemon zest in a medium bowl until smooth.
3. Spoon equal amounts of the ricotta mixture into the center of each puff pastry square. Fold the edges of the pastry up around the filling, creating a rustic tart shape. Brush the edges with the beaten egg.
4. After just 20 minutes in the oven, your pastry will transform into a golden brown and puffed delight. Once they've cooled slightly, you can proudly dust them with powdered sugar and garnish with fresh mint leaves, if desired, for a beautiful finish.

INGREDIENTS

- 1 cup ricotta cheese
- 1/4 cup honey
- 1 teaspoon vanilla extract
- 1/2 teaspoon lemon zest
- 1 sheet puff pastry, thawed
- 1 egg, beaten (for egg wash)
- 1 tablespoon powdered sugar (optional, for garnish)
- Fresh mint leaves (optional, for garnish)

NUTRITIONAL INFORMATION

290 calories, 7g protein, 29g carbohydrates, 16g fat, 1g fiber, 40mg cholesterol, 150mg sodium, 50mg potassium.

DARK CHOCOLATE-COVERED ALMONDS

DIRECTIONS

1. Prepare Almonds: Preheat oven to 350°F. Spread almonds on a baking sheet and roast for 5-7 minutes, until lightly browned and fragrant. Let cool.
2. Melt Chocolate: In a microwave-safe bowl, work your magic and melt the dark chocolate in 30-second intervals, stirring between each, until it's fully melted and smooth, a testament to your culinary prowess.
3. Coat Almonds: Add the roasted almonds to the melted chocolate and stir until they are evenly coated.
4. Set and Serve: Using a fork, transfer the chocolate-covered almonds to a parchment-lined baking sheet, spacing them apart. Sprinkle with sea salt if desired. Let the chocolate set at room temperature or refrigerate for quicker setting.

SERVES
4

PREP TIME
15

METHOD
Roasting

COOK TIME
5

INGREDIENTS

- 1 cup whole raw almonds
- 4 oz dark chocolate (70% cocoa), chopped
- 1/2 tsp sea salt (optional)

NUTRITIONAL INFORMATION

220 calories, 5g protein, 20g carbohydrates, 15g fat, 4g fiber, 0mg cholesterol, 20mg sodium, 220mg potassium.

OLIVE OIL COOKIES

SERVES
4

PREP TIME
15

METHOD
Baking

COOK TIME
12

DIRECTIONS

1. Preheat the oven to 350°F (175°C). Line a baking sheet with parchment paper.

2. In a medium bowl, whisk together the flour, sugar, baking powder, and salt. This will create the base for our tasty cookies. Whisk together the olive oil, egg, lemon zest, orange zest, and vanilla extract in another bowl. Gradually add the dry and wet ingredients, mixing until a dough forms.

3. Scoop tablespoon-sized portions of dough onto the prepared baking sheet, spacing them about 2 inches apart. Flatten each cookie slightly with the back of a spoon.

4. Bake for 12 minutes or until the edges are golden. Allow the cookies to cool on the baking sheet for 5 minutes before transferring them to a wire rack to cool completely.

INGREDIENTS

- 1 cup all-purpose flour
- 1/2 cup granulated sugar
- 1/4 teaspoon baking powder
- 1/4 teaspoon salt
- 1/4 cup extra-virgin olive oil

- 1 egg
- 1 tablespoon grated lemon zest
- 1 tablespoon grated orange zest
- 1 teaspoon vanilla extract

NUTRITIONAL INFORMATION

120 calories, 2g protein, 18g carbohydrates, 5g fat, 1g fiber, 15mg cholesterol, 70mg sodium, 30mg potassium.

MEDITERRANEAN ORANGE YOGURT CAKE

DIRECTIONS

1. Preheat and Prepare: Preheat your oven to 350°F. Grease a 9-inch round cake pan and line the bottom with parchment paper.
2. Mix Dry Ingredients: In a large bowl, whisk together the flour, sugar, baking powder, baking soda, and salt.
3. Combine Wet Ingredients: In another bowl, whisk together the Greek yogurt, eggs, olive oil, orange zest, orange juice, honey, and vanilla extract until well combined.
4. It's time to bring it all together! Gradually add the wet ingredients to the dry ingredients, stirring until they're just combined. Pour the batter into the prepared cake pan. Bake for 45 minutes or until a toothpick inserted into the center comes out clean. Now, the hardest part is to let the cake cool in the pan for 10 minutes before transferring to a wire rack to cool completely. You can do it!

SERVES
6

PREP TIME
15

METHOD
Baking

COOK TIME
45

INGREDIENTS

- 1 1/2 cups all-purpose flour
- 1/2 cup granulated sugar
- 1/4 cup honey
- 1/2 teaspoon baking powder
- 1/2 teaspoon baking soda
- 1/4 teaspoon salt

- 1 cup plain Greek yogurt
- 2 large eggs
- 1/3 cup olive oil
- Zest of 2 oranges
- 1/3 cup fresh orange juice
- 1 teaspoon vanilla extract

NUTRITIONAL INFORMATION

250 calories, 5g protein, 38g carbohydrates, 9g fat, 1g fiber, 40mg cholesterol, 160mg sodium, 100mg potassium.

CHAPTER 09
Sauces and Condiments

ZATZIKI

DIRECTIONS

1. Prepare the Cucumber: To prepare the cucumber, place the grated cucumber in a clean kitchen towel and gently squeeze out the excess moisture.

2. Mix Ingredients: In a medium bowl, combine the Greek yogurt, grated cucumber, minced garlic, lemon juice, olive oil, chopped dill, salt, and black pepper.

3. Combine and Chill: Mix until well combined. Cover and refrigerate for at least 30 minutes to allow the flavors to meld together.

4. Serve: Serve chilled as a dip with fresh vegetables on pita bread or as a sauce for grilled meats.

SERVES
4

PREP TIME
10

METHOD
NO-COOK

COOK TIME
0

INGREDIENTS

- 1 cup plain Greek yogurt
- 1 medium cucumber, peeled, seeded, and finely grated (about 1 cup)
- 2 cloves garlic, minced
- 1 tablespoon fresh lemon juice

- 1 tablespoon olive oil
- 1 tablespoon chopped fresh dill
- 1/2 teaspoon salt
- 1/4 teaspoon ground black pepper

NUTRITIONAL INFORMATION

60 calories, 3g protein, 5g carbohydrates, 3g fat, 0g fiber, 5mg cholesterol, 180mg sodium, 100mg potassium.

CLASSIC BASIL PESTO

DIRECTIONS

1. Place garlic, pine nuts, and basil leaves in a food processor and pulse until chopped finely.
2. Pulse a few more times after adding the Parmesan cheese.
3. Take your time and add the olive oil gradually and steadily while the food processor is operating, blending the pesto until it's thoroughly combined.
4. Season to taste with salt and pepper.

SERVES
4

PREP TIME
10

METHOD
NO-COOK

COOK TIME
0

INGREDIENTS

- 2 cups fresh basil leaves, packed
- 1/2 cup grated Parmesan cheese
- 1/2 cup extra-virgin olive oil
- 1/3 cup pine nuts

- 3 garlic cloves, minced
- 1/4 teaspoon salt
- 1/4 teaspoon freshly ground black pepper

NUTRITIONAL INFORMATION

230 calories, 3g protein, 4g carbohydrates, 23g fat, 1g fiber, 5mg cholesterol, 150mg sodium, 160mg potassium.

TAPENADE

DIRECTIONS

1. Combine the capers, garlic, Kalamata olives, green olives, and anchovy fillets in a food processor.
2. Pulse to chop roughly.
3. Pulse in the olive oil and lemon juice until a chunky mixture forms. Add more black pepper to taste.
4. Move to a serving bowl and serve as a condiment or with bread and crackers.

SERVES
4

PREP TIME
10

METHOD
NO-COOK

COOK TIME
0

INGREDIENTS

- 1 cup pitted Kalamata olives
- 1 cup pitted green olives
- 2 tablespoons capers, drained
- 2 cloves garlic, minced

- 4 anchovy fillets, drained
- 3 tablespoons fresh lemon juice
- 1/4 cup extra virgin olive oil
- 1/4 teaspoon black pepper

NUTRITIONAL INFORMATION

230 calories, 3g protein, 4g carbohydrates, 23g fat, 1g fiber, 5mg cholesterol, 150mg sodium, 160mg potassium.

MUHAMMARA

DIRECTIONS

1. Set the oven temperature to 400°F. After 20 minutes of roasting on a baking sheet, the skin of the red bell peppers should be blistered and blackened. Remove the peppers from the oven and allow them to cool. Remove the seeds, peel the skin, and cut.
2. Place the pomegranate molasses, breadcrumbs, roasted red bell peppers, lemon juice, cumin, smoked paprika, red pepper flakes, and minced garlic in a food processor.
3. Slowly pour the olive oil while the machine operates until the mixture is smooth and thoroughly blended. To taste, add salt and pepper for seasoning.
4. Transfer the mutton to a bowl for serving. Whether you choose to enjoy it right away or store it in the fridge for later, take a moment to appreciate the delicious dish you've prepared.

SERVES
4

PREP TIME
10

METHOD
Roasting

COOK TIME
20

INGREDIENTS

- 2 large red bell peppers
- 1 cup walnuts
- 1/4 cup breadcrumbs
- 2 tablespoons pomegranate molasses
- 1 tablespoon lemon juice
- 1 teaspoon ground cumin

- 1 teaspoon smoked paprika
- 1/2 teaspoon red pepper flakes
- 2 garlic cloves, minced
- 1/4 cup extra virgin olive oil
- Salt and freshly ground black pepper to taste

NUTRITIONAL INFORMATION

220 calories, 4 g protein, 14 g carbohydrates, 18 g fat, 4 g fiber, 0 mg cholesterol, 150 mg sodium, 200 mg potassium.

ROMESCO

DIRECTIONS

1. Place the toasted bread pieces, garlic cloves, roasted red bell peppers, and toasted almonds in a food processor. Pulse until chopped finely.
2. Include the smoked paprika, red wine vinegar, salt, and cayenne (if using). Mix thoroughly.
3. Slowly pour the olive oil while the machine runs until the mixture is smooth and emulsified.
4. Taste and, if needed, adjust the seasoning. Use it as a dip or sauce, perfect for serving with pita bread or as a spread on sandwiches.

SERVES
4

PREP TIME
15

METHOD
NO-COOK

COOK TIME
0

INGREDIENTS

- 3 roasted red bell peppers, peeled and seeded
- 1/2 cup almonds, toasted
- 2 garlic cloves
- 1/4 cup extra virgin olive oil
- 2 tablespoons red wine vinegar
- 1 slice of whole-grain bread, toasted and torn into pieces
- 1 teaspoon smoked paprika
- 1/2 teaspoon salt
- 1/4 teaspoon cayenne pepper (optional)

NUTRITIONAL INFORMATION

180 calories, 4 g protein, 10 g carbohydrates, 15 g fat, 3 g fiber, 0 mg cholesterol, 260 mg sodium, 200 mg potassium.

MEAL PLAN ADVICES

The number of calories a person should consume per day while following the Mediterranean diet varies based on several factors, including age, gender, weight, height, and activity level. Here is a general guideline:

Daily Caloric Needs by Activity Level

Sedentary (little or no exercise)
- Women: 1,800 to 2,000 calories
- Men: 2,200 to 2,400 calories

Moderately Active (moderate exercise 3-5 days a week)
- Women: 2,000 to 2,200 calories
- Men: 2,400 to 2,600 calories

Active (intense exercise 6-7 days a week)
- Women: 2,200 to 2,400 calories
- Men: 2,600 to 3,000 calories

Key Components of the Mediterranean Diet

- Fruits and Vegetables: Aim for at least 5 servings per day.

- Whole Grains: Include whole grains like brown rice, quinoa, and whole wheat bread.

- Healthy Fats: Focus on healthy fats from sources like olive oil, nuts, and avocados.

- Protein: Include lean proteins such as fish, poultry, legumes, and nuts.

- Dairy: Consume moderate amounts of dairy, preferably low-fat or fat-free options.

- Red Meat and Sweets: Limit red meat and sweets to occasional consumption.

- Wine: If you drink, do so in moderation, typically one glass of red wine per day.

In summary

Adjust the portion sizes and specific foods according to your personal caloric needs and preferences while maintaining the core principles of the Mediterranean diet. For personalized advice, consult with a registered dietitian or nutritionist.

30-DAY MEAL PLAN

DAY	BREAKFAST	LUNCH	SNACK	DINNER	DESSERT
1	Mediterranean Oatmeal	Greek Village Salad (Horiatiki)	Classic Hummus with carrot sticks	Grilled Salmon with Lemon and Dill	Mediterranean Orange Yogurt Cake
2	Tomato and Feta Toast	Lentil and Spinach Soup	Caprese Skewers	Mediterranean Baked Cod	Poached Pears in Red Wine
3	Greek Yogurt with Nuts and Honey	Chickpea and Spinach Salad	Grilled Halloumi	Shrimp Saganaki	Grilled Peaches with Greek Yogurt
4	Egg Scramble with Spinach	Mediterranean Beet Salad	Mushroom and Goat Cheese Crostini	Baked Red Snapper	Ricotta and Honey Tartlets
5	Sweet Pea and Ricotta Toast	Classic Minestrone Soup	Bruschetta with Tomato and Basil	Seafood Paella	Baked Apples with Cinnamon and Honey
6	Muesli with Skyr	Tabbouleh	Mediterranean Deviled Eggs	Salmon and Asparagus	Berry and Mint Salad
7	Savory Muffins with Olives and Feta	Greek Lemon Chicken Soup (Avgolemono)	Zucchini Fritters	Baked Cod with Tomatoes and Olives	Olive Oil Cookies
8	Simple Shakshuka	Watermelon and Feta Salad	Tapenade with whole-grain crackers	Baked Tilapia with Lemon	Dark Chocolate-Covered Almonds
9	Turkish Menemen	Mediterranean Cauliflower Salad	Pistachio and Pomegranate Muhammara	Fish and Vegetable Skewers	Olive Oil and Almond Cake
10	Mediterranean Egg Muffins	Mediterranean Vegetable Soup	Roasted Red Pepper Hummus	Lemon Garlic Mussels	Baked Figs with Honey and Almonds
11	Tomato and Feta Toast	Chickpea and Tomato Soup	Smoked Salmon and Cream Cheese Rolls	Grilled Swordfish Steaks	A piece of dark chocolate
12	Greek Yogurt with Nuts and Honey	Fig and Arugula Salad	Tzatziki with cucumber slices	Pan-Seared Scallops	Grilled Peaches with Greek Yogurt
13	Egg Scramble with Spinach	Roasted Pepper and Artichoke Salad	Caprese Skewers	Grilled Salmon with Lemon and Dill	Berry and Mint Salad
14	Sweet Pea and Ricotta Toast	Tuscan White Bean Soup	Classic Hummus with bell pepper slices	Mediterranean Baked Cod	Baked Apples with Cinnamon and Honey
15	Muesli with Skyr	Avocado and Quinoa Salad	Mushroom and Goat Cheese Crostini	Shrimp Saganaki	Mediterranean Orange Yogurt Cake

30-DAY MEAL PLAN

DAY	BREAKFAST	LUNCH	SNACK	DINNER	DESSERT
16	Savory Muffins with Olives and Feta	Spicy Moroccan Lentil Soup	Tapenade with whole-grain crackers	Baked Red Snapper	Olive Oil Cookies
17	Simple Shakshuka	Greek Village Salad (Horiatiki)	Zucchini Fritters	Seafood Paella	Orange Slices with Dark Chocolate
18	Turkish Menemen	Mediterranean Beet Salad	Bruschetta with Tomato and Basil	Salmon and Asparagus	Poached Pears in Red Wine
19	Mediterranean Egg Muffins	Greek Lemon Chicken Soup (Avgolemono)	Pistachio and Pomegranate Muhammara	Baked Cod with Tomatoes and Olives	Berry and Mint Salad
20	Tomato and Feta Toast	Chickpea and Spinach Salad	Tzatziki with cucumber slices	Baked Tilapia with Lemon	Grilled Peaches with Greek Yogurt
21	Greek Yogurt with Nuts and Honey	Classic Minestrone Soup	Salmon and Cream Cheese Rolls	Fish and Vegetable Skewers	Ricotta and Honey Tartlets
22	Egg Scramble with Spinach	Mediterranean Cauliflower Salad	Roasted Red Pepper Hummus	Lemon Garlic Mussels	Baked Figs with Honey and Almonds
23	Sweet Pea and Ricotta Toast	Chickpea and Tomato Soup	Mediterranean Deviled Eggs	Grilled Swordfish Steaks	A piece of dark chocolate
24	Muesli with Skyr	Tabbouleh	Caprese Skewers	Pan-Seared Scallops	Olive Oil and Almond Cake
25	Savory Muffins with Olives and Feta	Mediterranean Vegetable Soup	Classic Hummus with carrot sticks	Grilled Salmon with Lemon and Dill	Orange Slices with Dark Chocolate
26	Simple Shakshuka	Broccoli and Chickpea Salad	Mushroom and Goat Cheese Crostini	Mediterranean Baked Cod	Mediterranean Orange Yogurt Cake
27	Turkish Menemen	Watermelon and Feta Salad	Tapenade with whole-grain crackers	Shrimp Saganaki	Dark Chocolate-Covered Almonds
28	Mediterranean Egg Muffins	Mediterranean Beet Salad	Zucchini Fritters	Baked Red Snapper	Baked Figs with Honey and Almonds
29	Tomato and Feta Toast	Fig and Arugula Salad	Pistachio and Pomegranate Muhammara	Seafood Paella	Poached Pears in Red Wine
30	Greek Yogurt with Nuts and Honey	Avocado and Quinoa Salad	Tzatziki with cucumber slices	Salmon and Asparagus	Olive Oil Cookies

COOKING CONVERSION CHART

Volume Equivalents (liquid)

US STANDART	US STANDART (OUNCHES)	METRIC (APPROXIMATE)
2 tablespoons	1 fl. oz.	30 ml
1/4 cup	2 fl. oz.	60 ml
1/2 cup	4 fl. oz.	120 ml
1 cup	8 fl. oz.	240 ml
1 1/2 cups	12 fl. oz.	355 ml
2 cups or 1 pint	16 fl. oz.	475 ml
4 cups	32 fl. oz.	1 L
1 gallon	128 fl. oz.	4 L

Volume Equivalents (DRY)

US STANDART	US STANDART (OUNCHES)
1/2 teaspoon	2 ml
3/4 teaspoon	4 ml
1 teaspoon	5 ml
1 tablespoon	15 ml
1/2 cup	118 ml
3/4 cup	177 ml
1 cup	235 ml
2 cups or 1 pint	475 ml
3 cups	700 ml
4 cups or 1 quart	1 L
1 gallon	4 L

COOKING CONVERSION CHART

OVEN TEMPERATURES

WEIGHT EQUIVALENTS

FAHRENHEIT (F)	CELSIUS (C) (APPROXIMATE)	US STANDART	METRIC (APPROXIMATE)
250	120	1/2 ounce	15 g
300	150	1 ounce	30 g
325	165	2 ounces	60 g
350	180	4 ounces	115 g
375	190	8 ounces	225 g
400	200	12 ounce	340 g
425	220	16 ounces or 1 pound	455 g
450	230		

CONCLUSION

Congratulations on taking the first steps toward a healthier lifestyle with "The Mediterranean Diet Cookbook for Beginners." By now, you have explored the rich flavors, vibrant colors, and wholesome ingredients that define Mediterranean eating. This journey is about changing what you eat and embracing a holistic approach to living well.

The Mediterranean diet is more than a collection of recipes; it celebrates food, family, and tradition. It emphasizes fresh, seasonal produce, whole grains, lean proteins, and healthy fats, all while encouraging mindful eating and the joy of sharing meals with loved ones.

As you integrate these principles into your daily life, remember that the Mediterranean diet is not a rigid set of rules. It's a lifestyle that can be tailored to your individual tastes and needs. Feel free to explore new ingredients, try different recipes, and make this way of life uniquely yours.

More than just health benefits, the Mediterranean diet promotes a holistic approach to life. It's not just about what you eat, but also about physical activity, stress reduction, and a sense of community. These are all vital elements of a healthy and fulfilling life.

We hope this cookbook has inspired you to savor Mediterranean cuisine's delights and provided you with the tools to create delicious, nutritious meals at home. May your culinary adventures bring you and your loved ones joy, health, and vitality.

Thank you for choosing "The Mediterranean Diet Cookbook for Beginners." Here's to a future filled with flavorful, nourishing dishes and a vibrant, healthy lifestyle.

Bon appétit!

YOUR BONUS
Enjoy Cooking

Seasonal Eating Guide

Welcome to your Seasonal Eating Guide! Embrace the Mediterranean diet by enjoying fresh, seasonal produce all year round. This guide will help you choose the best fruits and vegetables for each season and delicious recipes from your cookbook.

Winter (December - February)

Seasonal Produce:
- Fruits: Citrus fruits (oranges, grapefruits, lemons), pomegranates, persimmons, kiwis
- Vegetables: Brussels sprouts, cabbage, kale, leeks, radishes, sweet potatoes, winter squash

Sample Recipe:

Roasted Winter Vegetables with Herbs
- Ingredients: Sweet potatoes, Brussels sprouts, carrots, olive oil, rosemary, thyme
- Instructions: Toss vegetables with olive oil, rosemary, and thyme. Roast at 400°F (200°C) for 25-30 minutes until tender and golden.

Tips:
- Use citrus fruits in salads and dressings to add a fresh, zesty flavor.
- Incorporate hearty vegetables like kale and cabbage into soups and stews.

Spring (March - May)

Seasonal Produce:
- Fruits: Strawberries, apricots, cherries, loquats, medlars
- Vegetables: Artichokes, asparagus, peas, fennel, radishes, spinach

Sample Recipe:

Spring Pea and Asparagus Salad
- Ingredients: Fresh peas, asparagus, red onion, mint, feta cheese, lemon juice, olive oil
- Instructions: Blanch peas and asparagus. Toss with thinly sliced red onion, chopped mint, crumbled feta, lemon juice, and olive oil. Serve chilled.

Tips:
- Enjoy fresh, raw vegetables in salads for a crisp, refreshing meal.
- Use herbs like mint and parsley to brighten up dishes.

Seasonal Eating Guide

Summer (June - August)

Seasonal Produce:

- Fruits: Watermelon, peaches, nectarines, figs, berries
- Vegetables: Tomatoes, cucumbers, eggplants, zucchini, bell peppers, green beans

Tips:

- Make the most of juicy, ripe tomatoes in salads, sauces, and bruschetta.
- Experiment with grilling fruits like peaches and figs for a unique dessert.

Fall (September - November)

Seasonal Produce:

- Fruits: Apples, pears, grapes, figs, pomegranates
- Vegetables: Pumpkin, butternut squash, sweet potatoes, mushrooms, Swiss chard

Autumn Harvest Salad

- Ingredients: Roasted pumpkin, arugula, apples, walnuts, goat cheese, balsamic vinaigrette
- Instructions: Roast pumpkin cubes until tender. Toss with arugula, thinly sliced apples, toasted walnuts, and crumbled goat cheese. Drizzle with balsamic vinaigrette.

Tips:

- Incorporate root vegetables and squash into hearty, warming dishes.
- Use apples and pears in both savory and sweet recipes for a seasonal touch.

Sample Recipe:

Mediterranean Grilled Vegetables

- Ingredients: Zucchini, eggplant, bell peppers, olive oil, balsamic vinegar, garlic, basil
- Instructions: Slice vegetables and marinate in olive oil, balsamic vinegar, and minced garlic. Grill until tender. Garnish with fresh basil.

Sample Recipe:

Enjoying Seasonal Produce

Eating seasonally ensures you get the freshest, most flavorful produce while supporting local agriculture. Use this guide to inspire your meals and explore each season's vibrant flavors.

RECIPE CARD

INGREDIENTS:

Serves   Prep   Cook

DIRECTIONS:

Notes

RECISE CARD

INGREDIENTS:

Serves   Prep   Cook

DIRECTIONS:

Notes

RECIPE CARD

INGREDIENTS:

YOI   🕐   🍲

Serves   Prep   Cook

DIRECTIONS:

Notes

Made in the USA
Middletown, DE
05 September 2024

60388986R00066